REAL PRESENCES

REAL PRESENCES

GEORGE STEINER

THE UNIVERSITY OF CHICAGO PRESS

The University of Chicago Press, Chicago 60637
Faber and Faber Limited. London
©1989 by George Steiner
All rights reserved. Published 1989
Printed in the United States of America

98 97 96 95 94 93 92 91 90   543

Library of Congress Cataloging-in-Publication Data

Steiner, George, 1929–
    Real presences.

    1. Languages—Philosophy.   2. Arts—Philosophy.
I. Title.
P106.S773 1989   401   89-4897
ISBN 0-226-77233-0

For Jacqueline Werly,
source of music.

Les preuves fatiguent la vérité.
[Proofs weary the truth.]
Georges Braque

When you are philosophizing
you have to descend into primeval chaos
and feel at home there.
Wittgenstein

CONTENTS

I   A SECONDARY CITY

We speak still of 'sunrise' and 'sunset'. We do so as if the Copernican model of the solar system had not replaced, ineradicably, the Ptolemaic. Vacant metaphors, eroded figures of speech, inhabit our vocabulary and grammar. They are caught, tenaciously, in the scaffolding and recesses of our common parlance. There they rattle about like old rags or ghosts in the attic.

This is the reason why rational men and women, particularly in the scientific and technological realities of the West, still refer to 'God'. This is why the postulate of the existence of God persists in so many unconsidered turns of phrase and allusion. No plausible reflection or belief underwrites His presence. Nor does any intelligible evidence. Where God clings to our culture, to our routines of discourse, He is a phantom of grammar, a fossil embedded in the childhood of rational speech. So Nietzsche (and many after him).

This essay argues the reverse.

It proposes that any coherent understanding of what language is and how language performs, that any coherent account of the capacity of human speech to communicate meaning and feeling is, in the final analysis, underwritten by the assumption of God's presence. I will put forward the argument that the experience of aesthetic meaning in particular, that of literature, of the arts, of musical form, infers the necessary possibility of this 'real presence'. The seeming paradox of a 'necessary possibility' is, very precisely, that which the poem, the painting, the musical composition are at liberty to explore and to enact.

This study will contend that the wager on the meaning of meaning, on the potential of insight and response when one human voice addresses another, when we come face to face with the text and work of art or music, which is to say when we encounter the *other* in its condition of freedom, is a wager on transcendence.

This wager – it is that of Descartes, of Kant and of every poet, artist, composer of whom we have explicit record – predicates the presence of a realness, of a 'substantiation' (the theological reach of this word is obvious) within language and form. It supposes a passage, beyond the fictive or the purely pragmatic, from meaning to meaningfulness. The conjecture is that 'God' *is*, not because our grammar is outworn; but that grammar lives and generates worlds because there is the wager on God.

Such a conjecture may, wherever it has been or is put forward, be wholly erroneous. If it is embarrassed, it will most certainly be so.

2

One of the radical spirits in current thought has defined the task of this sombre age as "learning anew to be human". On a more restricted scale, we must, I think, learn anew what is comprised within a full experience of created sense, of the enigma of creation as it is made sensible in the poem, in the painting, in the musical statement.

To do so, I want to start with a parable or rational fiction.

Imagine a society in which all talk *about* the arts, music and literature is prohibited. In this society all discourse, oral or written, about serious books or paintings or pieces of music is held to be illicit verbiage.

The sole book reviews in this imaginary community would be those which we find in the philosophical gazettes of the eighteenth and the quarterlies of the nineteenth century: dispassionate summaries of the new publication together with representative extracts and quotations. There would be no journals of literary criticism; no academic seminars, lectures or colloquies on this or that poet, playwright, novelist; no 'James Joyce quarterlies' or 'Faulkner newsletters'; no interpretations of, no essays of opinion on, sensibility in Keats or robustness in Fielding.

Texts would, where necessary, continue to be established and edited in the most rigorous, lucid form. This form is *philological*, a crucial term and concept which I want to articulate in this essay. What would be banned is the thousandth article or book on the true meanings of *Hamlet* and the article immediately following in rebuttal, qualification or augment. I am imagining a counter-Platonic republic from which the reviewer and the critic have been banished; a republic for writers and readers.

Correspondingly, there would be catalogues, reasoned and scrupulous, of an artist's *œuvre*, of art exhibitions, museums, public and private collections. Reproductions of the best quality would be readily available. But there would be an interdict on art criticism, on journalistic reviews of painters, sculptors and architects. There would be no further tomes on symbolism in Giorgione; no essays on the psyche of Goya or essays on these essays. Again, the order of comment allowed would be 'philological', which is to say of an explicative and historically contextual kind. The problem arising from the fact that all explication is, in some measure, evaluative and critical is, to be sure, a challenge.

At the heart of these prohibitions would be that on reviews, critiques, discursive interpretations (as opposed to analyses) of musical compositions. I believe the matter of music to be central to that of the meanings of man, of man's access to or abstention from metaphysical experience. Our capacities to compose and to respond to musical form and sense directly implicate the mystery of the human condition. To ask 'what is music?' may well be one way of asking 'what is man?' One must not flinch from such terms and from the fundamental semantic improprieties which they may entail. These elusive but also immediate categories of speech, of questioning, have their own imperative and clarity. The point is that these categories need to be lived before they can be stated.

Thus there would, in our fiction, be a prodigality of musical scores, of guides to performance and audition. There would be no overnight or weekly verdicts on new works, no verbal descriptions of the daemonic in Beethoven or of death wishes in Schubert. Where analysis is required, it would be of a pragmatic, anonymous sort. Once more, the enabling format would be that which I will seek to define and characterize as 'philological'.

In short, I am construing a society, a politics of the primary; of immediacies in respect of texts, works of art and musical compositions. The aim is a mode of education, a definition of values devoid, to the greatest possible extent, of 'meta-texts': this is to say, of texts about texts (or paintings or music), of academic, journalistic and academic-journalistic – today, the dominant format – talk about the aesthetic. A city for painters, poets, composers, choreographers, rather than one for art, literary, musical or ballet critics and reviewers, either in the market-place or in academe.

Would literature, music and the arts in this imaginary

6

community exist and evolve unexamined, unevaluated, disbarred from the energies of interpretation and the disciplines of understanding? Does the ostracism of high gossip (the German word *Gerede* conveys the exact tenor of busy vacancy) cause a blank and passive silence – silence can also be of the most active, answering quality – around the life of the creative imagination?

By no means.

3

The very question reflects our current *misère*. It tells of the dominance of the secondary and the parasitic. It betrays a radical misconception of the functions of interpretation and of hermeneutics. This latter word is inhabited by the god Hermes, patron of reading and, by virtue of his role as messenger between the gods and the living, between the living and the dead, patron also of the resistance of meaning to mortality. Hermeneutics is normally defined as signifying the systematic methods and practices of explication, of the interpretative exposition of texts, particularly scriptural and classical. By extension, such methods and practices apply to the readings of a painting, sculpture or sonata. Throughout this essay, I shall try to elucidate hermeneutics as defining the enactment of answerable understanding, of active apprehension.

The three principal senses of 'interpretation' give us vital guidance.

An interpreter is a decipherer and communicator of meanings. He is a translator between languages, between cultures and between performative conventions. He is, in essence, an executant, one who 'acts out' the material before him so as to give it intelligible life. Hence the third major sense of 'interpretation'.

An actor interprets Agamemnon or Ophelia. A dancer interprets Balanchine's choreography. A violinist a Bach partita. In each of these instances, interpretation is understanding in action; it is the immediacy of translation.

Such understanding is simultaneously analytical and critical. Each performance of a dramatic text or musical score is a critique in the most vital sense of the term: it is an act of penetrative response which makes sense sensible. The 'dramatic critic' *par excellence* is the actor and the producer who, with and through the actor, tests and carries out the potentialities of meaning in the play. The true hermeneutic of drama is staging (even the reading out loud of a play will, usually, cut far deeper than any theatrical review). In turn, no musicology, no music criticism, can tell us as much as the action of meaning which is performance. It is when we experience and compare different interpretations, this is to say performances, of the same ballet, symphony or quartet, that we enter the life of comprehension.

Observe the moral aspect (it will be fundamental to my case). Unlike the reviewer, the literary critic, the academic vivisector and judge, the executant invests his own being in the process of interpretation. His readings, his enactments of chosen meanings and values, are not those of external survey. They are a commitment at risk, a response which is, in the root sense, responsible. To what, save pride of intellect or professional peerage, is the reviewer, the critic, the academic expert accountable?

Interpretative response under pressure of enactment I shall, using a dated word, call *answerability*. The authentic experience of understanding, when we are spoken to by another human being or by a poem, is one of responding responsibility. We are answerable to the text, to the work of art, to the musical offering, in a very specific sense, at once moral, spiritual and psychological. It is the task of this study to spell out the implications of this threefold accountability. The immediate point is this: in respect of meaning and of valuation in the arts, our master intelligencers are the performers.

This is manifest of music, drama, ballet. It is less evidently the case in regard to non-dramatic literature. Yet here, as well, understanding can be made action and immediacy. Much great poetry, not only that of Pindar's *Odes* or the Homeric epics, but that of Milton, of Tennyson, of Gerard Manley Hopkins, calls for recitation. The meanings of poetry and the music of those meanings, which we call metrics, are also of the human body. The echoes of sensibility which they elicit are visceral and tactile. There is major prose no less focused on oral articulation. The diverse musicalities, the pitch and cadence in Gibbon, in Dickens, in Ruskin, are most resonant to active comprehension when read aloud. The erosion of such reading from most adult practices has muted primary traditions in both poetry and prose.

In reference to language and the musical score, enacted interpretation can also be inward. The private reader or listener can become an executant of felt meaning when he learns the poem or the musical passage by heart. To learn by heart is to afford the text or music an indwelling clarity and life-force. Ben Jonson's term, "ingestion", is precisely right. What we know by heart becomes an agency in our consciousness, a 'pace-maker' in the growth and vital complication of our identity. No exegesis or criticism from without can so directly incorporate within us the formal means, the principles of executive organization of a semantic fact, be it verbal or musical. Accurate recollection and resort in remembrance not only deepen our grasp of the work: they generate a shaping reciprocity between ourselves and that which the heart knows. As we change, so does the informing context of the internalized poem or sonata. In turn, remembrance becomes recognition and discovery (to re-cognize is to know

9

anew). The archaic Greek belief that memory is the mother of the Muses expresses a fundamental insight into the nature of the arts and of the mind.

The issues here are political and social in the strongest sense. A cultivation of trained, shared remembrance sets a society in natural touch with its own past. What matters even more, it safeguards the core of individuality. What is committed to memory and susceptible of recall constitutes the ballast of the self. The pressures of political exaction, the detergent tide of social conformity, cannot tear it from us. In solitude, public or private, the poem remembered, the score played inside us, are the custodians and remembrancers (another somewhat archaic designation on which my argument will draw) of what is resistant, of what must be kept inviolate in our psyche.

Under censorship and persecution, much of the finest in modern Russian poetry was passed from mouth to mouth and recited inwardly. The indispensable reserves of protest, of authentic record, of irony, in Akhmatova, in Mandelstam and in Pasternak, have been preserved and mutely published in the editions of personal memory.

In our own licensed social systems, learning by heart has been largely erased from secondary schooling and the habits of literacy. The electronic volume and fidelity of the computerized data bank and of processes of automatic retrieval will further weaken the sinews of individual memory. Stimulus and suggestion are of an increasingly mechanical and collective quality. Encountered in easy resort to electronic media of representation, much of music and of literature remains purely external. The distinction is that between 'consumption' and 'ingestion'. The danger is that the text or music will lose what physics calls its 'critical mass', its implosive powers within the echo chambers of the self.

Thus our imaginary city is one in which men and women practise the arts of reading, of music, of painting or sculpture, in the most direct ways possible. The great majority, who are themselves neither writers, nor painters, nor composers, will, so far as it lies in their capabilities and freedom, be respondents, answerers in action. They will learn by heart, perceiving the elemental pulse of love implicit in that idiom; knowing that the 'amateur' is the lover (*amatore*) of that which he knows and performs. The interpositions of academic-journalistic paraphrase, commentary, adjudication, have been removed. Interpretation is, to the largest possible degree, lived.

But does this mean, nevertheless, that criticism in the stricter sense, that considered arguments on aesthetic phenomena, on form and worth, are missing?

Again, a misconception is operative.

4

All serious art, music and literature is a *critical* act. It is so, firstly, in the sense of Matthew Arnold's phrase: "a criticism of life". Be it realistic, fantastic, Utopian or satiric, the construct of the artist is a counter-statement to the world. Aesthetic means embody concentrated, selective interactions between the constraints of the observed and the boundless possibilities of the imagined. Such formed intensity of sight and of speculative ordering is, always, a critique. It says that things might be (have been, shall be) otherwise.

But literature and the arts are also criticism in a more particular and practical sense. They embody an expository reflection on, a value judgement of, the inheritance and context to which they pertain.

No stupid literature, art or music lasts. Aesthetic creation is intelligent in the highest degree. The intelligence of a major artist can be that of sovereign intellectuality. The minds of Dante or of Proust are among the most analytic, systematically informed, of which we have record. The political acumen of a Dostoevsky or a Conrad is difficult to match. Witness the theoretical rigour of a Dürer, of a Schoenberg. But intellectuality is only one facet of creative intelligence; it need not be dominant. More than ordinary men or women, the significant painter, sculptor, musician or poet relates the raw material, the anarchic prodigalities of consciousness and sub-consciousness to the latencies, often unperceived, untapped before him, of articulation. This translation out of the inarticulate and the private into the general matter of human recognition requires the utmost crystallization and investment of introspection and control. We lack the right word for the extreme energizing and governance of instinct, for the ordered enlistment of intuition, which mark the artist. That intelligence of the highest strength, be it lodged in the sculptor's hands drumming on a table or in Coleridge's dreams, is at work, is obvious. How could this intelligence not also be critical of its own products and of its precedent? The readings, the interpretations and critical judgements of art, literature and music from within art, literature and music are of a penetrative authority rarely equalled by those offered from outside, by those propounded by the non-creator, this is to say the reviewer, the critic, the academic.

Let me give examples.

Virgil reads, guides our reading of, Homer as no external critic can. The *Divine Comedy* is a reading of the *Aeneid*, technically and spiritually 'at home', 'authorized' in the several and interactive senses of that word, as no extrinsic commentary by one who is himself not a poet can be. The presence, visibly solicited or exorcized, of Homer, Virgil and Dante in Milton's *Paradise Lost*, in the epic satire of Pope and in the pilgrimage upstream of Ezra Pound's *Cantos*, is a 'real presence', a critique in action. Successively, each poet sets into the urgent light of his own purposes, of his own linguistic and compositional resources, the formal and substantive achievement of his predecessor(s). His own practice submits these antecedents to the most stringent analysis and estimate. What the *Aeneid* rejects, alters, omits altogether from the *Iliad* and the *Odyssey* is as critically salient and instructive as that which it includes via variant, *imitatio* and modulation. The Pilgrim's gradual dissociations from his Master and guide towards the close of Dante's *Purgatorio*, the corrections made of the *Aeneid* in the citations from and references to it in the *Purgatorio*, constitute the closest of critical readings. They tell of the felt limits of the classical in regard to Christian revelation. There is no critical-academic equivalent.

Joyce's *Ulysses* is a critical experiencing of the *Odyssey* at the level of general structure, of narrative instruments and rhetorical particularity. Joyce (like Pound) reads Homer with us. He reads him through the rival refractions not only of Virgil or of Dante, but through the sheer critical intelligence of his own inventions of echo, of his own over-reaching design of derivation. Unlike that of the critic or academic expositor, Joyce's reading is answerable to the original precisely because it puts at eminent risk the stature, the fortunes of his own work.

Such acts of criticism and of self-criticism within the critical motion perform the pre-eminent function of all worthwhile reading. They make the past text a present presence. It is this vitalizing assessment of past presentness, together with the critical prevision of its claims on futurity (now, says Borges, *Ulysses* comes prior to and foretells the *Odyssey*), which defines just insight. In the poet's criticism of the poet from within the poem, hermeneutics reads the living text which Hermes, the messenger, has brought from the undying dead.

Other examples crowd to mind. Literary-academic criticism of George Eliot's *Middlemarch* is distinguished (see F. R. Leavis). Our imagined culture will, however, subsist without it. What will matter will be its ability to recognize the primary critique of *Middlemarch* in *The Portrait of a Lady*. A felt apprehension of how the latter grew out of the former, of the ways in which Henry James's narrative organization and dramatized psychology are a re-thinking, a comprehensive re-reading of George Eliot's flawed masterpiece; a grasp of the manner in which the coda of *The Portrait of a Lady* fails to resolve the implausibilities of motive and conduct which James had registered in the *dénouement* to *Middlemarch* – these will make us party to a critical act of the first order. The one novel comes to live in and against the other. As in Borges's quip, chronology becomes reversible. We learn to read *Middlemarch* in the probing light of James's treatment; we then return to *The Portrait of a Lady* and come to recognize the transformative inflections of its source. These inflections are not parasitical as in the case of purely critical, pedagogical commentary and verdict. The two constructs of imagination enter into fertile 'contra-diction'.

The secondary literature on *Madame Bovary* is legion and expendable. Biographical, stylistic, psychoanalytic, deconstructive commentaries have been brought to bear on almost every paragraph of Flaubert's text. But in our 'answerable' city, it is to another novel that we turn for creative interpretation and assay. *Anna Karenina* is, in the full connotations of the word, a 're-vision' of Flaubert. Tolstoy's breadth and spontaneity of present-ment, the gusts of vital disorder which blow through the great narrative blocs, argue a fundamental critique of Flaubert's willed, sometimes choking perfection. The force of religious inference in *Anna Karenina* makes us critically responsive to the genius of reduction in Flaubert's invention (a genius already noted by Henry James when he spoke of Emma Bovary as "too small a thing").

In short: criticism is energized into creative responsibility when Racine reads and transmutes Euripides; when Brecht reconstrues Marlowe's *Edward II*; when, in *The Maids*, Genet plays his sharp variations on the themes of Strindberg's *Miss Julie*. The most useful criticism I know of Shakespeare's *Othello* is that to be found in Boito's libretto for Verdi's opera, and in Verdi's response, both verbal and musical, to Boito's suggestions. Cruelly, perhaps, it does seem to be the case that aesthetic criticism is worth having only, or principally, where it is of a mastery of answering form comparable to its object.

One further category of answering form ought to be cited. Translation is, as we have seen, interpretative in its very etymology. It is also critical in the most creative ways. Valéry's transposition of Virgil's *Eclogues* is critical creation. No critical study of the surge and limits of the baroque quite matches Roy Campbell's translations from the Spanish of St John of the Cross. No literary criticism will educate our inner ear to the changing music of meaning in the English language as will a reading of successive versions of Homer in the translations by Chapman, Hobbes, Cowper, Pope, Shelley, T. E. Lawrence and Christopher Logue. Each of these argues in action a critical experience not only of the Homeric epics and hymns, but a critical response to previous versions and to the distance travelled in the history of spoken language and sensibility. This illumination extends to the special guise of translation we call parody. Set Pope's Homer (which is, after Milton, the eminent English epic poem) next to the Greek original. Consider both in 'triangulation' with those passages in *The Rape of the Lock* which, point-to-point, travesty

15

passages in the *Iliad*. The mutual interplay which results is one of the high moments of critical intelligence and imagining.

The obstacles to worthwhile art and music criticism are of the essence. What has language, however adroitly used, to *say* in regard to the phenomenology of painting, of sculpture, of musical structure? How can the *modus operandi* of a picture or sonata be verbalized at all? In even the most reputed of academic-literary criticism of the fine arts and of music, the prevalence of elevated chit-chat, the pathos of a fundamental (ontological) absurdity, are palpable. Why should our 'city of the primary' bother?

Let us look first at the arts.

The material of interpretation and of judgement is, in the main, provided by artists. It is their *maquettes* and sketches, it is, to a necessarily limited degree, their letters and journals (Delacroix's, Paul Klee's) which make accessible to us the incipience of purposed form. It is successive states of a carving, of an engraving, which yield some insight into the genesis of meaning. Grammatical-logical discourse is radically at odds with the vocabulary and syntax of matter, with that of pigment, stone, wood or metal. Berkeley hints at this contrariety when he characterizes matter as one of "the languages of God". If at all, speech is edged in reach of materiality, this is to say, in educative reach of that which must, finally, be left unsaid, in the notations made by artists and craftsmen.

It is nearly unjust to confront even the best of critical writings on art, such as Diderot's, Ruskin's or Longhi's, with the letters of Van Gogh or Cézanne. It is these letters that reveal what words can of the translation of matter into sense; it is they that take us, some way at least, into the workshop of bringing-into-being. The dynamics implicit in a creator's record and evaluation of his own works are, rigorously, psychosomatic: internal vision

16

and muscle, pre-conscious compaction and willed, technical externalization, are indivisible. It is, most generally, before this fusion that language falters. There are exceptions: in Keats's letters, in Nadezhda Mandelstam's minute notice of Mandelstam's gestures of finding. But these are rare.

In the polity which I am proposing, any man or woman open to the over-reaching of his own personal life, which we call the experience of the poetic and the arts, will want to commit to joyous memory passages from Van Gogh's letters to his brother, Theo, or from Cézanne's reports to fellow artists and friends of work in progress. These documents do, in some measure, make us privy to the mystery. 'Mystery' is a term crucial to the argument. It is not to be flinched from, but it is to be close-pressed for its necessity and definition.

In painting and sculpture, as in literature, the focused light of both interpretation (the hermeneutic) and valuation (the critical-normative) lies in the work itself. The best readings of art are art.

This is, most literally, the case where painters and sculptors copy previous masters. It is true, in graduated degrees, where they incorporate, quote, distort, fragment or transmute motifs, passages, representational and formal configurations, from another painting or sculpture into their own. It is these vitalizing responsions which our citizens of the immediate will look for.

Such incorporation and reference, conscious or unconscious, mimetic or polemic, is constant in art. Art develops via reflection of and on preceding art, where 'reflection' signifies both a 'mirroring', however drastic the perceptual dislocation, and a 're-thinking'. It is through this internalized 're-production' of and amendment to previous representations that an artist will articulate what might appear to have been even the most spontaneous, the most realistic of his sightings. Goya's sketches of the frenetic violence of the Madrid uprising against Bourbon and Napoleonic rule are, in demonstrable fact, replete with gestural motifs, with conventions of iconographic and symbolic shorthand, transposed from his own earlier compositions and those of other artists, mainly of a pastoral or mythological genre. This in no way impugns the passionate integrity of Goya's witness. It simply shows the degree to which an artist's perception of an event or scene is itself an 'art-act'. I borrow this term from linguistic philosophy where 'speech-act' is current. It simply shows how naturally an artist's 'criticism of life' is also art criticism in the most vivid and magisterial sense.

It is, moreover, where art is most innovative, most iconoclastic in manifesto and execution, that its judgements of other art are most compelling. We have no more persuasive guidance to Ingres than in certain drawings and paintings by Dali. Our finest critic of Velázquez is Picasso. Indeed, almost the sum of Picasso's protean devices can be seen as a series of critical re-valuations of the history of Western and, at certain moments, of 'primitive' art. Similarly, Dürer's re-thinking of the Flemish masters, the patient meditation on the planes and volumes of Piero della Francesca in Cézanne, Manet's performative investigations of Goya, Monet's Turner, are art criticism and assessment enacted, and unmatched in their acumen.

The question as to whether anything meaningful can be *said* (or written) about the nature and sense of music lies at the heart of this essay. This question does seem to me to imply not only fundamental speculations as to the limits of language; it takes us to the frontiers between conceptualization of a rational-logical sort and other modes of internal experience. More than any other act of intelligibility and executive form, music entails differentiations between that which can be understood, this is to say, paraphrased, and that which can be thought and lived

18

in categories which are, rigorously considered, transcendent to such understanding. More narrowly: no epistemology, no philosophy of art can lay claim to inclusiveness if it has nothing to teach us about the nature and meanings of music. Claude Lévi-Strauss's affirmation that "the invention of melody is the supreme mystery of man" seems to me of sober evidence. The truths, the necessities of ordered feeling in the musical experience are not irrational; but they are irreducible to reason or pragmatic reckoning. This irreducibility is the spring of my argument. It may well be that man is man, and that man 'borders on' limitations of a peculiar and open 'otherness', because he can produce and be possessed by music.

When it speaks of music, language is lame. Customarily, it takes refuge in the pathos of simile. There are kindlings of discursive revelation in Plato, in Kierkegaard, in Schopenhauer, Nietzsche and Adorno. There is a rare force of suggestion in the definition proposed by Gioseffo Zarlino, the principal Renaissance theoretician of music: music "mingles the incorporeal energy of reason with the body". One grasps but does not grasp Schopenhauer's famous dictum: that music "exhibits itself as the metaphysical to everything physical in the world. . . We might, therefore, just as well call the world embodied music as embodied will." In music, Pierre Jean Jouve, the French poet and essayist, locates "the Promise", this is to say, the concrete universal of the challenging and consoling experience of the unfulfilled. The messianic intimation in music is often manifest. But attempts to verbalize it produce impotent metaphors. One of the best qualified teachers of music and musical analysts in our time, Hans Keller, dismissed all musicology and music criticism as phoney.

This fundamental issue has direct bearing on our citizens of the immediate. In music, at a more radical level than in either literature or the arts, the best of intelligence, interpretative and critical, is musical. Asked to explain a difficult *étude*, Schumann sat down and played it a second time. We have already noted that the most 'exposed', therefore engaged and responsible act of musical interpretation, is that of performance. In ways closely analogous to those we have cited in texts, paintings or sculptures, the criticism of music truly answerable to its object is to be found within music itself. The construct of theme and variation, of quotation and *reprise*, is organic to music, particularly in the West. Criticism is, literally, instrumental in the ear of the composer.

Almost cruelly, we can contrast the communicative wealth of the musical with the waste motions of the verbal. The singular concision of complex moods in Chopin defies discourse. It is made explicit in Busoni's variations. But these variations are also a critique in the finest sense: the tonal strengths of the Busoni version point out certain complacencies in Chopin's ready art. Consider the critical authority in Mozart's rearrangements and reorchestrations of *Messiah*; in Beethoven's ten variations, at once attentive and critically magisterial, on a duet from Salieri's *Falstaff*. Liszt's transcriptions for piano from Italian opera, from classical symphonies, from the compositions of his contemporaries, notably Wagner, go a long way to suggest that Liszt's was the foremost critical (if not self-critical) tact in the history of Western music. Together, these transcriptions make up a syllabus of enacted criticism. The musical-cultural literature on the involvements of Wagnerian opera in the politics of our century is mountainous. Does it define and set out the question at as concise and impassioned a depth as do the citations from *Tristan und Isolde* in Shostakovich's Fifteenth Symphony – citations which not only force us back to the matter of Wagner, but which throw an unsparing critical light on the tragic politics of Shostakovich himself and of his society?

One last example. Verbally, it is very nearly impossible to arrive at any satisfactory concept of the coming of 'modernism' into music. The clearest critical expositions of this turn are to be found in Schoenberg's transcriptions and orchestrations of earlier masters, such as Bach and Brahms. Correspondingly, the argument on modernity is made both existential and critical in Stravinsky's metamorphic variants on Gesualdo, on Pergolesi. In ways unavailable to verbal commentary, these *reprises* are, simultaneously, modernistic ironizations and de-mythologizations of modernity. Simultaneously, they regroup the lines and fields of force in our musical inheritance, and they 'make new'. Such regrouping and innovation is, *par excellence*, the function and justification of criticism.

Thus, structure is itself interpretation and composition is criticism. In our Utopia of lived literacy, critical, evaluative intelligence would be plainly heard and put to responsive use by anyone making music and by all who choose to listen actively. Here again, the discrimination between an active and a passive silence recurs. No critic from without, no instant reviewer would, in our city, be licensed to package the central offerings and demands of musical experience.

5

The fantasy which I have sketched is only that. The prohibition of secondary discourse on literature and the arts would demand an implausible degree of censorship. Not even the most rudimentary of structures of literacy and of musical reception is, one imagines, free from critical or didactic interposition. In the domain of the aesthetic, one cannot legislate for immediacy.

There are, moreover, counter-arguments to my entire scheme. There is scholarship, interpretation and criticism of art, music, literature, there is even (though very rarely) reviewing which has legitimate claims to the dignity of creation. No commonsense canon of sensibility would want to erase Samuel Johnson or Coleridge on Shakespeare; Walter Benjamin on Goethe; or Mandelstam's essay on Dante. How can one demarcate the secondary from the primary, the parasitic from the immediate in Reynolds's *Discourses*, in Erwin Panofsky's readings of medieval and Renaissance art and iconography? Should even the most convinced commitment to the first-hand rule out of court the analyses, the critical evocations of music by Berlioz, by Adorno (who composed), by a virtuoso and musicologist such as Charles Rosen? In letters, especially, the borderlines are uncertain and dynamic. By force of style, of energized analogy, hermeneutics and evaluation can enter into the sphere of the primary text. We re-read Hazlitt on certain theatrical performances, we re-read Henry James on Turgenev or Maupassant. In rare but luminous instances, even the festive oration or academic encomium – Dostoevsky on Pushkin, Thomas Mann on Schiller – takes on the answerable autonomy of the poetic.

The examples I have cited are, almost entirely, derived from artists on art, writers on writing and musicians, either composers or executants, on music. But both in theory and (rare) practice, there can be liberating interpretation and enduring assessment by those who only respond. The pleasures and accuracies of perception would be the poorer if we did not have books such as Erich Auerbach's *Mimesis* or William Empson on *The Structure of Complex Words* (Empson was, to be sure, a minor but distinctive poet).

My censorious fiction can also be rebuked on a more modest level. Where is the harm?

The great bulk of literary journalism and reviewing, of literary-critical essays, of art and music criticism, is totally ephemeral. It moulders into oblivion the morning after. Tomes of academic explication and judgement – on Milton's rhetoric, on carnality in Baudelaire, on the semantics of wit in the early, the middle or the later Shakespeare, on the deeps of Dostoevsky – are soon out of print and sepulchred in the decent dust of deposit libraries. Critical schools, academic reading lists, semiotic programmes for the interpretation of the arts, come and go like querulous shadows. The continued production of works of exegesis and of criticism on authors, painters, sculptors and composers, already analysed and classed a hundredfold, does afford transient pleasure, benign illusions of significance and, with luck, a certain professional niche and modest revenue for all manner of secondary souls (how could I not know and acknowledge this to be so?).

What would the first novelist, the débutant performer, the painter previously unexhibited, do without the reviewer? For many a tentative reader, the pedagogic-critical shepherd can be invaluable. Why deprive a culture of this tributary current and of the nourishment, however meagre, however short-lived, which it may carry to the great tides of creation? Surely there must be some licence under God for caring mediocrity.

All this is perfectly true. Yet my fantasy of abstention does have its purpose. It aims to direct close attention to dominant characteristics in our present encounters with aesthetic creation. My parable would urge a fundamental question: that of the presence or absence in our individual lives and in the politics of our social being, of *poiesis*, of the act and experienced act of creation in the full sense. What is the ontological status (no other epithet is accurate), the 'status of being' and of meaning, of the arts, of music, of the poem, in the present city? This question can and, in the first instance, must be put in terms which are those of aesthetics, of psychology and of cultural politics. Inevitably, however, it will entail a further dimension.

6

The usages and values predominant in the consumer societies of the West today are the opposite to those in the imaginary community of the immediate. It is the secondary and the parasitic which overwhelm. Literate humanity is solicited daily by millions of words, printed, broadcast, screened, about books which it will never open, music it will not hear, works of art it will never set eyes on. A perpetual hum of aesthetic commentary, of on-the-minute judgements, of pre-packaged pontifications, crowds the air. Presumably, the greater part of art-talk or literary reportage, of music reviews or ballet criticism, is skimmed rather than read, heard but not listened to. None the less, the effect is antithetical to that visceral, personal encounter and appropriation designated by Ben Jonson. There is little "ingestion"; it is the 'digest' that prevails.

At the level of critical-academic interpretation and evaluation, the volume of secondary discourse defies inventory. Not even the computer and the electronic data bank are able to cope. No bibliographies are up to date. The mass of books and critical essays, of scholarly articles, of *acta* and dissertations produced each day in Europe and the United States, has the blind weight of a tidal wave. In the 'humanities' – a general rubric which I will take to encompass literature, music, the arts together with the totality of hermeneutic and normative argument which they occasion – enumeration verges on the grotesque.

If I give a number of summary examples, it is only because

the reader-consumer outside the academy and the art and music worlds has little idea of the pertinent dimensions.

In the field of modern literature alone, Russian and Western universities are thought to register some thirty thousand doctoral theses *per annum*. An average college or university library will need to stock some three to four thousand periodicals in the humanities. These include learned and critical journals on poetry, drama and fiction; musicological and music-critical journals; quarterlies and research bulletins in the history and criticism of the fine arts. Periodical publications in theoretical and formal aesthetics multiply. The several thousand learned societies, specialized associations, organizations of literary historians, musicologists, friends of *belles-lettres*, art historians, students of the ballet, of the theatre, of one or another style in architecture, of the history and semiology of film which appear on UNESCO lists, which publish the proceedings of their passions in a more or less official and regular format, are the iceberg tip. No computer has indexed the newsletters, annual *memorabilia*, minutes of the covens which celebrate this or that rite of explication.

Where major figures or bodies of work are at issue, interpretative and critical 'coverage' – a suggestive word – defies listing. The fullest bibliography we have of books and articles on Goethe's *Faust* runs to four stately tomes. It was incomplete when it appeared and is now out of date. It has been estimated that, since the late 1780s, some twenty-five thousand books, essays, articles, contributions to critical and learned colloquia, doctoral dissertations, have been produced on the true meanings of *Hamlet*. No register that we have of Dante commentaries, of expository and critical opinions on the philosophic, structural, contextual aspects of the *Divine Comedy*, can be regarded as exhaustive. Some thirty-five learned congresses marked the

Victor Hugo centennial of 1985. Their *acta* are in course of publication.

But lesser masters, and contemporary writers and artists whose intrinsic stature remains arguable, have become the object of academic-critical mass assembly. Even prior to the foundation of a journal and of newsletters devoted wholly to his work, Faulkner had been the subject of more than one thousand scholarly articles and theses. Commentaries on Ezra Pound, on Samuel Beckett, are pouring off the conveyor belt. A mandarin madness of secondary discourse infects thought and sensibility.

Periods, climates of culture, in which the exegetic and the critical dominate, are called 'Alexandrine' or 'Byzantine'. These epithets refer to the prevalence of grammatological, editorial, didactic, glossarial and judiciary techniques and ideals over any actual poetic-aesthetic creativity in Hellenistic Alexandria and in the Byzantium of the later Empire and Middle Ages. They tell of the imperialism of the second- and third-hand. The name of no single metropolis can designate what is analogous to Alexandria, to Byzantium, in our present situation. Perhaps our age will come to be known as that of the marginalists, of the clerics in the market.

What are the causes? Who, to borrow Homer's myth of dishevelment and waste, has untied the wind-bags of Aeolus? I am not certain that there is any wholly satisfactory answer.

The genius of the age is that of journalism. Journalism throngs every rift and cranny of our consciousness. It does so because the press and the media are far more than a technical instrument and commercial enterprise. The root-phenomenology of the journalistic is, in a sense, metaphysical. It articulates an epistemology and ethics of spurious temporality. Journalistic presentation generates a temporality of equivalent instantaneity. All things are more or less of equal import; all are only daily.

Correspondingly, the content, the possible significance of the material which journalism communicates, is 'remaindered' the day after. The journalistic vision sharpens to the point of maximum impact every event, every individual and social configuration; but the honing is uniform. Political enormity and the circus, the leaps of science and those of the athlete, apocalypse and indigestion, are given the same edge. Paradoxically, this monotone of graphic urgency anaesthetizes. The utmost beauty or terror are shredded at close of day. We are made whole again, and expectant, in time for the morning edition.

Each of these principles and tactics is antinomian to serious literature and the arts. The temporalities of poetry, art and music are not only specific to themselves (music is, indeed, time made free of temporality). The text, the painting, the composition are wagers on lastingness. They embody the *dur désir de durer* ('the harsh, demanding desire for durance'). In a perfectly concrete sense, their deadlines are those of an unknown extension into the future. Serious art, music, writing is not *interesting* in the sense in which journalism must be. Its solicitation and governance of us are those of a patient necessity. The appeal of the text, of the work of art or music is, radically, *disinterested*. Journalism bids us invest in the *bourse* of momentary sensation. Such investment yields 'interest' in the most pragmatic sense. The dividends of the aesthetic are, precisely, those of 'disinterest', of a rebuke to opportunity. Above all, meaningful art, music, literature are not new, as is, as must strive to be, the news brought by journalism. Originality is antithetical to novelty. The etymology of the word alerts us. It tells of 'inception' and of 'instauration', of a return, in substance and in form, to beginnings. In exact relation to their originality, to their spiritual-

27

formal force of innovation, aesthetic inventions are 'archaic'. They carry in them the pulse of the distant source.

Why then the prodigality of journalistic notice expended on the aesthetic?

Strictly considered, the claims of journalism to men's works and days are totalitarian. Journalism would 'cover' the sum total of happenings. In so far as they do 'happen', although in this context the very notion of occurrence is fundamentally impertinent, art, literature, music, dance are grist to the paper-mill. The mass media employ marriage counsellors and astrologers. Why should they not employ art critics and music reviewers?

But this is not the full answer by any means. Manifold accommodations between aesthetic consumption and political-social power, between leisure and industrialization, are relevant. The assumption of parliamentary and bureaucratic control by the educated bourgeoisie in the 1830s and 1840s dissociates the greater part of literary, artistic and musical patronage from the aristocratic and ecclesiastical élite of an *ancien régime*. Art, letters, music must now compete for response in the emporia of middle-class taste. Such competition compels notice and publicity. In his *Illusions perdues*, Balzac, who was among the very first to analyse and master the new instrumentalities, gives us a classic account of the changes. Advertisement and dissemination through journalism reach into every aspect of the aesthetic.

The consequence is a peculiar dialectic of false immediacy. Every day, in the urban centres, the new consumer – the middle-class reader, spectator, concert-goer, visitor of art galleries – is directed towards possible objects of perception and valuation. At the same time, he is 'distanced' from the goods displayed. His personal involvement in the text or painting or symphony, his potential investment in risks of consciousness, are mundanely gauged. An appreciation of music, of the arts, of letters is now a widely disseminated attribute of gentility and conspicuous leisure. Note the kindred connotations of augmented worth, of psychological and material profits, in the very word 'appreciation'. But there has been a crucial interposition. The journalistic or periodical reviewer and critic are the middlemen, the jobbers, the keepers of salutary distance between the anarchic, counter-utilitarian claims and subversions of the aesthetic on the one hand, and the prudential liberalities of the civic imagination on the other. They are the privileged, though in many ways scorned, couriers between realms of value which have need of each other – the arts do help fill the menacing spaces of private emptiness – but those aims are fundamentally adverse. The media do enable the poet and artist to declare his presence, to bruit his wares amid competing clamour. Reciprocally, the treatment of the arts and literature in the media informs, and informs reassuringly, the necessary public. The infernal machine of questioning vision and of mystery is defused by intermittence. Via the distance created by the book review or piece of musical criticism, the patron can patronize.

Speculatively, one could probe further. Again, it is the bourgeois revolutions, political and industrial, of the first half of the nineteenth century which are seminal. During and after these revolutions, literature, music and the arts, reviewed, academicized, glazed over by the daily and weekly press, came to be a partial surrogate for certain modes of political action. For Plato, a true adult is one whose discourse bears on the laws and politics of his city. In the life of the literate middle classes in modern industrial societies, such bearing is indeed institutionalized (in the ballot, in the right of candidacy to elected office). But it is also fitful, coming only occasionally. With the exponential anonymity and technicality of public functions, personal commitment to the political has become a more or less stale manoeuvre of delegation. Talk about culture, cultured talk, talk about such talk – 'have you read this morning's book review?', 'have you seen what the pundits say of the world genius of Bacon and the decline of Henry Moore?' – fills a certain political vacuum. It diverts, both in the sense of deflection and of entertainment.

In the humanities and liberal arts, however, it is not journalism *strictu sensu* which is the dynamo of the secondary. It is the academic and that immensely influential, although complex form, the academic-journalistic. It is the universities, the research institutes, the academic presses, which are our Byzantium.

The annexation of the living arts and literatures by the scholastics is a fascinating story. The transmutation of poetics into texts, this is to say, the lexical, grammatical, compositional analysis of a piece of literature, and the uses of such analysis towards rhetorical, civic and moral instruction, is as old as are the commentaries on Homer in ancient Greece. In essence, there is scarcely one among our interpretative-critical methods – the gloss, the footnote, the emendation, the recension of various readings, the critical paraphrase – which was not practised by the ancient Academy and Alexandria. Cicero's heuristic, mimetic and critical treatments of the Greek legacy constitute the binding model for the scholastic-academic enterprise of the humanities in the West. Taken over, intensified by the Byzantine grammarians and the Church Fathers, these theories and pragmatics of right reading, of hermeneutic explication, of editorial-critical discourse on discourse, organize the concept of the canonic, the drawing up of the syllabus, as these obtain to this day.

Little in the business of our schooling in letters, music and the arts, in that of our lectures and seminars, would seem alien to the minds of St Jerome or St Augustine. The evolution of classical and medieval means of understanding into modern philology and modern hermeneutics during the seventeenth, eighteenth and early nineteenth centuries is one of close-knit continuity. As is the deepening of textual inquiry from Spinoza's *Tractatus theologico-politicus* to the interpretative methodology of Schleiermacher. The Muses have always had entrance in academe.

But in the modern context, that entrance has become problematic. We have seen that secondary discourse on the aesthetic, both interpretative and critical, takes over from scriptural and theological exegesis its essential methodological and practical instruments. At the same time, the modern explicator-critic reverts to the elucidation and assessment of secular, mundane texts, works of art, musical compositions, such as had been practised by classical and Hellenistic grammarians, pedagogues and scholiasts. This twofold motion of immediate theological inheritance and of reversion to the aesthetic initiates ambiguities of the most opaque and consequential kind. I shall be considering these later.

The point at issue now is the expansionism of the academic-critical vision; of its territorial extension from the canonic to the contemporary.

With rare exceptions, textual commentary of an academic cast is, during the Renaissance, the Enlightenment and most of the nineteenth century, brought to bear on the presiding genius of the Greco-Roman source. The very notion of philology and 'higher criticism', where the claim to elevation is shared by scriptural and classical studies, intimates the editing, teaching and comparative explication of the classical. There is criticism of contemporaneous art, music and letters. But even at its gravest reach, in Samuel Johnson's *Lives of the Poets*, in Lessing's *Hamburgische Dramaturgie*, such criticism defines itself as of the

31

periodical-journalistic domain. It does not aspire to, it often contemns, the academic.

The erosion of this vital distinction is recent. It directs us towards deep-lying changes of structure in our modernity and in the force of Americanization so characteristic of this modernity. American higher education imports, at the turn of our century, the pedagogic programmes, the ideals of graduate study and doctoral research, the bibliographic orientation towards the secondary, of the German university system. The latter had been formulated and institutionalized by Wilhelm von Humboldt in Berlin, and by the charismatic mandarins of Iena and Göttingen. Though on a scale of unprecedented generosity and recruitment, American university seminars, institutes for humanistic research and criteria of professional incorporation through learned publication, are exponents of the nineteenth-century German ideal of academic humanism.

But with a difference. The German model was classical in focus and hierarchical in its identification of the pertinent syllabus. Democracy is, fundamentally, at odds with the canonic. Two principal impulses energize the American spirit: immanence and egalitarianism. The crux of American time is now. The past matters in direct reference to its usability in and by the present. American sensibility tends to invest remembrance not in historicity but in Utopia. Transcendence itself is made pragmatic; the definition of tomorrow is that of the empirical realization of substantive dreams. No other culture has so dignified the immanent.

Concomitantly, the egalitarian ideal seeks to domesticate excellence. The European canon orders vertically, gives differing ranks to the products of intellect and of feeling. Its strategies are those of exclusion. The Parnassus, the Pantheon of official glory, integral to European humanities, are suspect to American

32

sentiment. The American genius would democratize eternity. It follows that contemporary art, literature, music, dance have full rights of citizenship in the hermeneutic-critical responsibilities of the academy. The lines of demarcation between the academic and the journalistic, between intemporality and the daily, between *auctoritas*, as it articulates the sovereignty of the canonic precedent, and the experimental and ephemeral, are effaced. Identical techniques of commentary, themselves increasingly standardized and 'scientific', as is the tenor of American life, are applied to ancient and modern, to the established and the transitory.

Answering to the needs and hopes of a matchlessly inclusive and diverse society, the American university lays claims to totality as sweeping as those of journalism. No textuality, no art form, no mayfly of literary, musical or material contrivance is, *a priori*, ruled out of court. The appetite for exposition, instruction and taxonomy is omnivorous. The bell wether of American universities assigns to its 'core curriculum', this is to say, to its minimal requirements for literacy, a course on black women novelists of the early 1980s. Poets, novelists, choreographers, painters of the most derivative or passing interest, are made the object of seminars and dissertations, of undergraduate lectures and post-doctoral research. The axioms of the transcendent in the arts of understanding and of judgement – axioms which this essay seeks to clarify – are invested in the overnight.

In turn, the living writer, composer, choreographer or sculptor, the maker of films or ceramics, is invited into the academy. The American university does not only study and teach the living arts: it houses them in 'creative writing' programmes, workshops and recital rooms. Aristotle does not only look at the bust of Homer, as in Rembrandt's allegory of

33

the relations between the poetic and the philosophical-critical modes of being. He is now host to both the poet and the sculptor.

Two concepts call for reflection. That of 'research' into the humanities on the one hand; that of the co-habitation of the living arts and of the hermeneutic-academic on the other.

The aims of textual criticism, in its historical sense, were straightforward. The corpus of revealed and classical texts had to be properly edited. It was towards this precise end that humanistic-academic scholarship developed and cultivated the disciplines of philology, emendation, recension and lexical-grammatical annotation. In this context, 'research' had its exact meaning. It signified a systematic inquiry into the provenance, status, relative worth and interrelations of codices, manuscripts and preceding editions. What is the situation today?

In regard to musical scores, a good deal remains to be authoritatively edited, dated and formally analysed. Art history and iconography also provide further justification for historical and technical investigation, for documented attribution and 'reasoned publication', in the sense in which that phrase is used by those who first describe rigorously a previously unknown or mistaken art object.

In literary studies, which are the power-house of secondary discourse, the position is different. No doubt, there is a sense in which no edition, however learned and scrupulous, is ever perfect. No doubt, this or that pot-shard of textual or biographical information can still be fitted into the established reconstruction. But these are luxuries. Generally speaking, the texts in the canon of Western poetry, drama and fiction, from the *Iliad* and the *Odyssey* to *Ulysses* (a challenging case) or *The Magic Mountain*, have been adequately and more than adequately edited. The opulent minutiae of the *variorum* now extend to Proust and Rilke. As further works gain roots in the syllabus of the indispensable, they too will be 'textualized' critically by those philologists and text critics (rarer, said A. E. Housman, than are either poets or major critics) equipped for this exigent craft.

Currently, however, 'research' has pre-empted a far wider realm. In the academic treatment of the humanities, the fiftieth article on, say, metaphor in Scott Fitzgerald, on the narrative grace of Chaucer, on E. M. Forster's avoidance of the tragic, will be funded, presented and classified as research. The same applies to dissertations on writers already entombed in pyramids of paraphrase and opinion. In actual fact, such books, articles and theses are statements of personal intuition, of personal taste, more or less novel, more or less ingenious or productive of debate. Even where they exhibit unusual accuracies of feeling and elegance of proposal, these acts of secondary discourse are not 'research'. It is worth noting, furthermore, that such accuracy and elegance belong only to the very few. The entire notion of research in modern letters is vitiated by the evidently false postulate that tens of thousands of young men and women will have anything new and just to say about Shakespeare or Keats or Flaubert. In truth, the bulk of doctoral and post-doctoral 'research' into literature, and the publications which it spawns, are nothing more than a grey morass.

The dilution, the trivialization of the concept of research in the humanities, and the regimen of the parasitic which it sustains in our culture, has two causes. The first is the professionalization of the academic pursuit and appropriation of the liberal arts. Transposed from a European to an American setting, this enterprise took on industrial *élan*. Where there are no longer enough classical and eminent texts to be edited, there are always enough to be 're-valued'. Where knowledge of Greek and Latin, of Old and Elizabethan English ebbs, there are always contemporary authors available for academic teeth to grind.

35

The second motive is that of the humanistic imitation of the scientific. In their scale of bureaucratic formalization, of funding, in their eager pretence to theoretical rigour and cumulative discovery, the humanities in our universities and institutes of advanced studies strive obsessively to rival the high good fortunes of the exact and the applied sciences. This striving, and the mendacious notion of research which it entails, are themselves founded in the positivism and 'scientism' of the nineteenth century. They ape the aspirations to exact *Wissenschaft* – 'knowledge that is scientific', 'insight that is somehow verifiable as are scientific hypotheses' – as we find them in Comte, in Ranke. The fantastic success of the mathematical and the natural sciences, their prestige and socio-economic preferment, have mesmerized humanists and literati.

The sciences do proceed by research. In science, work of the very first order can be collective and cumulative. Scientific papers do bring new recognitions and methods in a demonstrable or refutable sense. In the laboratory, in the mathematical seminar, central techniques of perception and manipulation can be taught. Not one of these three configurations is genuinely applicable to aesthetic study and pronouncement, except at the most formal, linguistic-textual level. The positing of an opinion about a painter, poet or composer is not a falsifiable proceeding. In the humanities, collective formulations are almost invariably trivial (what worthwhile book after the Pentateuch has been written by a committee?). Nor is the process of insight cumulative and self-corrective, except in the most severely defined areas of textual philology, iconography, or musicology. The finest of later literary interpretation and criticism does not supersede Aristotle on Euripides, Samuel Johnson on *King Lear* (we may differ drastically from that unsettling reading, but we cannot refute or supersede it), or Sainte-Beuve on Racine. In the

36

speculative intuitions of the aesthetic, the motions of spirit are not those of an arrow, but of the spiral at once ascendant and retrogressive as is the stairway in the library of Montaigne.

Thirdly, critical tact, answerability to poetic and artistic shaping, can be exemplified but not taught. Their transmission from one generation to the next cannot be systematized as can be the handing on of scientific techniques and results.

Thus, in all but the strictly philological-historical area, the fabrication of humanistic 'research' is precisely that. The illusions which have resulted in the academy are calamitous.

The question of the incorporation inside universities of the arts and of living artists is less clear.

The material benefits for the recipients of academic bounty are obvious. The poet, playwright, composer, *cinéaste*, gets room and board, a workshop, a captive audience. For its part, academe profits from exposure to innovation, to anarchic vitality and the leaven of bad manners. It witnesses work in progress. The presence of the sculptor challenges that of the plaster casts in the art department. The poet-on-campus may, obliquely, induce salutary scepticism as to the nobility and altruism of past masters.

The negative aspects are subtler. Intimacies between the process of creation and that of analytic-discursive reflection are not native. Constrained by the very ambience of academic hospitality to a deliberate practice of self-awareness and self-explanation, the painter-in-residence, the poet in the seminar, the composer at the lectern, will find himself ousted from the exigent isolation, from the inchoate dynamics, opaque to himself, of his calling. The welcoming scrutiny he receives can render him falsely transparent.

Even where he is not a guest on campus, today's poet, artist or composer is, as never before, under pressure of academic attention and expectations. Consciously or not, numerous poets

– Auden being among the first to have registered and explored the damaging paradox – begin to write the type of poem that will reward the structural analyses of college and university classes. The novelist patterns for ambiguities, for polysemic densities of the kind prized and 'taught' by the explicator. Housing the vestigial claims of the psychoanalytic, art and literature departments in the university look to the Freudian or Jungian yield from painting and poem. Consciously or not, the creator labours to oblige. Distorting courtesies of reception obtain between artist and explainer. To a degree which is difficult to determine, the esoteric impulse in twentieth-century music, literature and the arts reflects calculation. It looks to the flattery of academic and hermeneutic notice. Reciprocally, the academy turns towards that which appears to require its exegetic, cryptographic skills. The text solicits 'adoption' by the university syllabus and reading list. The term is revealing; for the paternity thus obtained is, indeed, a false one.

The Saturn of explication devours that which it adopts. Or, more precisely, it makes it servile. Everywhere around us, at this period in Western culture, the aesthetic shows signs, and more than signs, of being 'academic'. The pejorative aura of that epithet now carries a twofold meaning. A growing measure of our aesthetic invention and response is academic precisely because it is of and for the academy.

The Byzantine dominion of secondary and parasitic discourse over immediacy, of the critical over the creative, is itself a symptom. An anxious desire for interposition, for explicative-evaluative mediation between ourselves and the primary, permeates our condition. To cite Byron's mocking distinction, we prefer reviewers to bards; or, rather, we cultivate those bards who are most reviewable, who 'can be taught'. Observe the semantic duplicity: poets who can be taught are also teachable.

The central source of the triumph of the secondary is the crux of my argument.

I shall be arguing that we crave remission from direct encounter with the 'real presence' or the 'real absence of that presence', the two phenomenologies being rigorously inseparable, which an answerable experience of the aesthetic must enforce on us. We seek the immunities of indirection. In the agency of the critic, reviewer or mandarin commentator, we welcome those who can domesticate, who can secularize the mystery and summons of creation. What intelligible meaning we can attach to these notions needs to be shown. Before proceeding to this decisive but most resistant stage of the argument, I want to consider the formal and historical relations between the created and the discursive. Is there not in the limitless proliferation of the secondary an inevitability? Am I tilting at windmills?

7

Commentary is without end. In the worlds of interpretative and critical discourse, book, as we have seen, engenders book, essay breeds essay, article spawns article. The mechanics of interminability are those of the locust. Monograph feeds on monograph, vision on revision. The primary text is only the remote font of autonomous exegetic proliferation. The true source of Z's tome are X's and Y's works on the identical topic. In both rhetorical conventions and substance, secondary texts are about secondary texts. Books of literary interpretation and criticism, of art criticism and musical aesthetics, are about previous books on the same or closely cognate themes. Essay speaks to essay, article chatters to article in an endless gallery of querulous echo. At present, in fact, the principal energies and animus of the academic-journalistic outpouring in the humanities is of a tertiary order. We have texts about the possibility and epistemological status of preceding secondary texts. There was, for example, Wordsworth. Thereafter came the flood of comment on Wordsworth. Today, the ardour burns in the paper on the semantic possibilities or impossibilities of writing about Wordsworth. Our talk is about talk, and Polonius is master.

How can personal sensibility go upstream, to the living springs of 'first being'? Does such an image of the primal have any legitimacy? This question arises, fundamentally, at three moments in the Western tradition.

In Judaism, unending commentary and commentary upon commentary are elemental. Talmudic exegesis exfoliates into uninterrupted study of and commentary on the Talmud. The lamps of explication must burn unquenched before the tabernacle. Hermeneutic unendingness and survival in exile are, I believe, kindred. The text of the Torah, of the biblical canon, and the concentric spheres of texts about these texts, replace the destroyed Temple. The dialectical movement is profound. On the one hand, there is a sense in which all commentary is itself an act of exile. All exegesis and gloss transports the text into some measure of distance and banishment. Veiled in analysis and metamorphic exposition, the *Ur*-text is no longer immediate to its native ground. On the other hand, the commentary underwrites – a key idiom – the continued authority and survival of the primary discourse. It liberates the life of meaning from that of historical-geographical contingency. In dispersion, the text is homeland.

The *Gemara*, the commentaries on the *Mishna*, the collection and collocation of oral laws and prescripts which, together, make up the Talmud; the *Midrash*, which is that part of the interpretative commentary which attends specifically to the interpretation of scripture, are both formally and substantively interminable. The *midrashic* method of reading is that of the argumentative, qualifying, revisionary gloss and marginalia on the holy text and on previous readings. Hermeneutical investigation bears on every level of possible meaning: semantic, grammatical, lexical. Formidably schooled memorization and philological virtuosity perform a dance of the spirit in front of the partially closed but radiant Ark of the letter.

This reading without end represents the foremost guarantee of Jewish identity. Unwaveringly minute study of the Torah is enjoined before any other rite or obligation. Dialogue with the ultimately, but only ultimately, unfathomable text is the breath of Jewish history and being. It has proved to be the instrument of improbable survival. At the same time, the Talmudic genius and method have, very possibly, generated within Judaic sensibility certain philological-legalistic sterilities and circularities. The dance turns never-endingly on itself. It is not only the Mosaic prohibition against images and the immemorial Jewish diffidence in the face of the act of creation which have, until very recently, made of the Jew a scholar-commentator rather than a shaper of aesthetic form (as he was, incomparably, when the Psalms, when the Song of Songs, when the Book of Job and Ecclesiastes came into being). It is the inherent ideal and practice of the secondary in respect of the revealed word. Most significantly, the greatest of modern Jewish writers and imaginers, Kafka, gives to his fictions the lineaments of exegesis, of probing, baffled marginalia to the abyss of meaning.

The rabbinic answer to the dilemma of the unending commentary is one of moral action and enlightened conduct. The hermeneutic exposition is not an end in itself. It aims to translate into normative instruction meanings indwelling in the manifold

41

previsions of the sacred message. As centuries pass, the Torah is not only preserved literally. It is safeguarded from the threat of the past tense. The ever-unfolding commentary provides the prescriptive, commemorative, metaphoric and esoteric components of the passage under scrutiny, of the single word or letter under loving disputation, with a palpable presentness. The gloss insists on pertinence here and now. Simultaneously, elucidation and conjecture prepare the passage for a future harvest. Via ever-renewed interpretations, this very same biblical verse, this very same parable, shall, in times and places of need as yet unknown, deploy illuminations and practical, existential applications as yet unperceived.

The contrast with Kabbalistic readings is instructive. The Kabbalist would translate understanding not into action but into final illumination. He seeks bedrock. Seven times seven are the strata of signification in the word, in the letter. Finalities of meditation, ecstatic attendance on darkness, may come within reach of the last secrets of sense, of those letters of white fire which speak the meaning of meaning. Such knowing is self-contained. It need not, it cannot be transposed into the imprecise contour of personal or communal behaviour. The reading is the crucial act and the Kabbalist remains boundlessly acquiescent in silence.

Both these modes of interpretative experience in the face of meaning, that of answerability compelling action, and that of pure receptivity, will have bearing on the concept of the encounter with presence.

The second moment in which the relations between the primary and the secondary, between the inspired and the discursive, are argued in depth, is that of medieval scholasticism. Self-replicating and variant, the helix of scholastic commentary winds around the stem of the scriptural and patristic canon. Our whole theme is made emblematic by a sequence of celebrated twelfth-century titles: Anselm of Laon's *Glossa ordinaria* on the Psalms and the Pauline Epistles is followed by Gilbert de la Porrée's *Media glossatura*; the latter, in turn, leads to Peter Lombard's *Magna glossatura*. The fine-nerved severities of formal analysis, the branching nuances of grammatical-semantic probing in the arts of reading of medieval schoolmen, no longer are a part of general or, indeed, privileged literacy. If they were, much in recent semiotics and grammatology would seem derivative from that earlier phenomenology and methodology of extreme scruple. Specifically, we would recognize in today's idolatry of the 'informational', of classificatory logistics and data storage, an almost parodistic fulfilment of the encyclopaedic lust in the medieval spirit, of that omnivorous appetite for a *summa*, for a *summa summarum* of the writ, glossed, annotated world.

This appetite, together with the postulate of a fourfold and ascending scale of understanding, from the literal and the moralizing, to the allegorical and the anagogical or purely spiritual – a scale without which the drama of organization in Dante's *Commedia* would have been inconceivable – begets unending commentary. Scholastic and clerical authorities were acutely aware of the dilemma. They observed the revealed text bending under the weight of ever-proliferating interpretation, paraphrase and glossarial elaboration. Deep-sea divers tell of a certain depth at which the human brain becomes possessed of the illusion that natural breathing is again possible. When this happens, the diver removes his helmet and drowns. He is inebriate with a fatal enchantment called *le vertige des grandes profondeurs*, 'the vertigo of the great deeps'. Masters of scholastic reading and explication knew this dizziness.

Hence the systematic and legislative attempts at agreed finality. The primary had to be protected from the choking growth of the secondary. Papal and councillary efforts were made to determine the true and everlasting meanings of the revealed. Note the radical difference between Catholic and Judaic textuality. There is no temporal singularity, no enigma of historicity ('why in this one place, why at that one time?') in the Judaic sense of the Creation and of the Mosaic reception and transmission of the Law. There is a strict, utterly mysterious temporality in the coming and ministry of Christ. Being so naturally, if inexplicably, immersed in actual time, the meanings of that coming, the normative consequences of the sayings of Christ and of the writings of the Apostles, must, as it were, be stabilized in eternity. The Torah is indeterminately synchronic with all individual and communal life. The Gospels, Epistles and Acts are not.

To achieve finalities of meaning one must punctuate (the very term is that of the 'full stop'). One must arrest the cancerous throng of interpretations and re-interpretations. The explicative and legislative decrees promulgated by Rome and by the custodians of orthodoxy in medieval Paris, the doctrinal-metaphysical enclosedness of Aquinas's *Summa*, can be understood as a series of attempts at hermeneutic 'end-stopping'. In essence, they proclaim that the primary text can mean *this* and *this*, but not *that*. The equations which relate rational comprehension and explicative authority to revelation are complex, but finally soluble. Thus dogma can be defined as hermeneutic punctuation, as the promulgation of semantic arrest. Orthodox eternity is the precise contrary of the unendingness of interpretative revision and commentary. In scholastic faith, logic and grammatology (as, later, in Hegel), eternity is ordinance and closed form. Unendingness is Satanic chaos.

It follows that heresy can be defined as 'un-ending re-reading' and revaluation. Heresy refuses exegetic finality. No text is *ne varietur*. The heretic is the discourser without end. His re-interpretations and revisions, his novel translations, even where they profess, strategically, a return to the authentic source, even where they allege that the understanding of the primary text will be made plainer and more relevant to the needs of an unstable world, generate an open-ended, disseminative hermeneutic. The Roman Catholic warning that interpretation without end, even where it claims to be 'fundamentalist' and textually reductive, will modulate, first, into historical criticism, next into more or less metaphoric deism and, lastly, into agnosti-cism, is logically and historically valid. Where it is without finiteness, secondary discourse is schismatic.

In both the Talmudic and the scholastic models of encounter with revealed and inspired meaning, the postulate of revelation is itself transcendent. The struggle against the secondary is one that would inhibit the relativization of the absolute. The third trial of methodological and applied insight into the relations between primary and secondary orders of enunciation, of felt form, is resolutely secular.

The logic, the motor principle of free association, on which the theory and practice of psychoanalysis depend, are those of an infinite series. Each unit in the associative chain does not only connect horizontally and in linear sequence with the next; it can itself become the starting point for an unbounded set of new linked connotations, associations and recall. The analyst's decision to interrupt the unwinding progression, to punctuate what is, in the most direct sense, an unending phrase, at the close, say, of sixty minutes or before the summer break, is arbitrary. The next association, now unvoiced, the next image-cluster, might, in fact, have proved to be the crucial one, the clue to deeper findings. It is this contingent, purely conventional practice of interruption which made Wittgenstein uneasy about the entire psychoanalytic enterprise.

Freud's paper of 1937 on "Terminal and Endless Analysis" seeks to confront the dilemma. Freud acknowledges that neurotic symptoms and manifestations recur long after the close of therapy. He concedes that the concept of the termination of the psychoanalytic process of verbal associations has no theoretical foundation. The only reasonable answer, therefore, is pragmatic and professional. "The termination of analysis is, I take it, a matter of *praxis*." The analytic sessions may be said to have been completed when the volume and supposed centrality of deciphered significations and memories allow a better integration of the speaker's ego (allow a more orderly and inclusive decoding of the text or the painting). It is characteristic of Freud's sovereign nonchalance in regard to the problematic nature of language itself – language being at once the raw material and sole instrument of all Freudian psychoanalysis – that he neither observes nor seeks to elucidate the underlying issue of semantic unendingness. "This procedure of free association and so on is queer, because Freud never shows us how we know where to stop," says Wittgenstein in his posthumously published conversations. Freud cannot show this. The filaments of associative congruence, of occlusions, of covert or declared suggestions, are limitless. As is the generation of sentences. Correspondingly, the process of psychoanalytic decoding and reading in depth can have no intrinsic or verifiable end. There is always more to be said about the poem or the picture or the buried intentionalities and self-betrayals of the musical composition (though psychoanalysis is almost helpless in regard to music, a point to which I want to return). There are always further layers to be excavated, deeper shafts to be sunk into the manifold strata of subconscious inception. The archaeology of sense is as

46

vertical, it is as much directed towards the *de profundis*, as is that of Talmudic exegesis from which so much of the spirit of Freud's hermeneutics was derived. Knowing no dogmatic terminality, psychoanalytic commentary on literature and the arts, its re-interpretation of precedent psychoanalytic readings – witness the tertiary literature on Freud's explications of Shakespeare, of Michelangelo, of Leonardo, of Dostoevsky or of Poe – are without end.

In a most graphic way, this automatism of secondary and tertiary discourse, this formal and empirical interminability as we see it in psychoanalytic pursuits of meaning, is illustrative of all interpretative and critical treatment of the aesthetic. By the logic of dialectical inversion ('dialectical' is an awkward but, here, inescapable term), the very methodologies and techniques which would restore to us the presence of the source, of the primary, surround, suffocate that presence with their own autonomous mass. The tree dies under the hungry weight of the vines.

8

The customary ways in which we experience the aesthetic in our twentieth-century culture, the customary ways in which we verbalize such experience – and it is the correspondence between the experience and the verbalization which I am seeking to clarify – are opposite to the ideals of immediacy, of personal engagement and answerability, which I sketched at the outset. The imbalance between the secondary and its object, between the 'text', which I take to include the art object, the musical composition, the dance, and the explicative-evaluative commentary they occasion, is very nearly grotesque. Parasitic discourse feeds upon living utterance; as in microbiological food-chains, the parasitic in turn feeds upon itself. Criticism, meta-criticism, dia-criticism, the criticism of criticism, pullulate.

The mechanics of inflation, which preside over so much that is characteristic of the political history, social crises and entrepreneurial energies in our century, are decisively functional in the humanities and in our individual relations to art, music, literature. It is less, perhaps, Byzantium and Alexandria which typify our condition than it is the Weimar of the 1920s. The underlying simile is worth looking at closely.

Each day, via journalism, via the journalistic-academic, the inherent value, the productive powers, the savings embodied in a creative currency, this is to say in the vitality of the aesthetic, are devalued. The paper Leviathan of secondary talk not only swallows the prophetic (there is prophecy and the prophecy of remembrance in all serious poetic and artistic invention): it spews it out diminished and fragmented. In the absence of the guarantor, a counterfeit mode of exchange, that of the review speaking to the review, of the critical article addressing the critical article, circulates endlessly. It is not, as Ecclesiastes would have it, that "of making many books there is no end". It is that 'of making books on books and books on those books there is no end'.

I have hinted that the consequences of trivia, however voluminous, can themselves be regarded as trivial. The mush-rooming of semantic-critical jargon, the disputations between structuralists, post-structuralists, meta-structuralists and decon-structionists, the attention accorded both in the academy and the media to theoreticians and publicists of the aesthetic – all these carry within their bustling pretence the germs of more or less rapid decay. "Fashion is the mother of death" (so Leopardi). It can be argued that the sepulchre, heaped around the primary text by exegesis and criticism, is made of ephemeral plaster.

48

The inflation of the parasitic is halted when the constructs of spuriousness collapse under their own weight, when the zero-point of trust and of felt meaning is reached. The declining fortunes of Marxist and psychoanalytic methods of decoding would appear to point in that direction. The parodistic lexica and grammatologies of Rabelais, Molière's *Précieuses ridicules* swept away with one gust of laughter – laughter being, at crucial times, another name for the seriousness of good sense – rhetorics, spectral systems and mandarin sabbaths as portentous, as condescending of true creation, as any now abroad. The essential idiom of the poem, of the piece of music, of the painting or sculpture is that of survival.

I question this consoling argument. I do so because I believe that the eclipse of the humanities, in their primary sense and presentness, in today's culture and society, implicates that of the humane.

We flinch from the immediate pressures of mystery in poetic, in aesthetic acts of creation as we do from the realization of our diminished humanity, of all that is literally bestial in the murderousness and gadgetry of this age. The secondary is our narcotic. Like sleepwalkers, we are guarded by the numbing drone of the journalistic, of the theoretical, from the often harsh, imperious radiance of sheer presence. Beauty can, indeed, be 'terribly born', as Yeats says. The cry of those Angels in Rilke's *Duino Elegies* can embarrass intolerably. The news brought by annunciations not only stays new; it can be unendurable in its ambiguity. So we slide past the singing rocks, their song stifled, or made artifice, by secular gloss and critique.

I sense that we shall not come home to the facts of our unhousedness, of our eviction from a central humanity in the face of the tidal provocations of political barbarism and technocratic servitude, if we do not redefine, if we do not re-

49

experience, the life of meaning in the text, in music, in art. We must come to recognize, and the stress is on *re*-cognition, a meaningfulness which is that of a freedom of giving and of reception beyond the constraints of immanence.

To argue this, to make it even worth serious disagreement, I must look insistently at the relations between language and the boundaries of language on the one hand, and the nature of aesthetic statement and experience on the other. I must, even if only provisionally, consider the intimate complementarities between an authentic act of reading, an authentic motion of answerability to music and to art, and the rights to human privacy, to the wholly personal hospitality we owe our own death – rights and an indebtedness now under pressure of narcotic devaluation in a culture of the secondary.

The pertinent categories of inference and felt intelligibility are theological and metaphysical. But they inhere in language. My case can only be made if I can render plausible a view of language and of meaning, of the limits of language in regard to certain orders of meaning, which differs from the views now most generally held and practised. An argument on our inward and our social being, with particular reference to the encounter with immediacy and transcendence in the aesthetic, is, of necessity, an argument on *Logos* and word.

II THE BROKEN CONTRACT

1

Anything can be said and, in consequence, written about *anything*. We scarcely pause to observe or to countenance this commonplace. But an enigmatic enormity inhabits it.

Every other human instrument and performative capability has its limitations. It is just conceivable that the mile will, at some future date, be run in three minutes. It is inconceivable, for reasons grounded in the neuro-physiology of the human animal, that it will be run in, say, three-quarters of a minute. Each and every corporeal capacity of the species is organically bounded. This boundary-condition is cardinal to life itself. Remarkable longevity in this or that individual is on record; but death is terminal at a fairly circumscribed upper limit. Thus in respect of personal existence and personal consciousness, at least so far as we have evidence, time and being, and the sum of time which being experiences, are finite.

Only language knows no conceptual, no projective finality. We are at liberty to say anything, to say what we will about anything, about everything and about nothing (the latter is a particularly striking and metaphysically intriguing licence). No deep-lying grammatical constraint, if any such can indeed be shown to obtain, abrogates the anarchic ubiquity of possible discourse. Nor does the pragmatic impracticality or, more accurately, the mechanical awkwardness of the generation of 'an endless sentence'. There may indeed be such sentences in the unvoiced, inward monologue of the deaf-mute and the autistic. Writing, also, offers what comes very near to being a disproof of the impossibility of the unending: in the *libido scribendi* of Sade's prose, punctuation marks are nothing more than a pause for breath, scornfully conceded, in a language-act which aims to exhaust, to exploit devouringly, the entirety of the sensory sets, series and combinations latent in imagining. When Wittgenstein's *Tractatus* declares the limits of language to be those of our world(s), it uses 'limits' tautologically. Language need halt at no frontier, not even, in respect of conceptual and narrative constructs, at that of death.

Translated into saying – where the notion of 'translation', of some pre-verbalized status is one of the most demanding uncertainty – the conceptual process, the deed of imagining, can abolish, reverse or confound all categories (themselves embedded in language) of identity and of temporality. Speech can change the rules under which it operates in the course of its operation, "making the green one red". This is to say that it can redraft every definitional and relational procedure, making of itself what linguists call 'an idiolect'. It then becomes a singular, unrepeatable message susceptible neither of re-use nor of demonstrable decipherment. This is the way 'single pad' codes operate in diplomatic or military cryptography. But this is also the motion towards perfect uniqueness, towards the absolute and seamless indivisibility between form and content elemental in the vocabulary and syntax of all serious poetry. Where, in the strictest sense, such autonomy – and 'autonomy' means, very precisely, the condition of being a law unto and only unto itself – is achieved, the meaning of the utterance or text will be understood only by its emitter. Yet this fact in no way invalidates its communicative, as distinct from its social or utilitarian, integrity. It is very probably to ourselves, and in a dialect unique to the final privacies of our psyche, that we say what matters most. It is, moreover, the self-transformative liberty in all

54

semantic codes, of which language is the foremost, that underlies every kind of philosophic scepticism and every epistemological critique of the innocence of relations between word and world.

Inside grammar, future tenses, optatives, conditionals are the formal articulation of the conceptual and imaginative phenomenality of the unbounded. What logic and grammatology define as 'the counter-factual' tells of a capacity absolutely central and specific to man (should this capacity not fill us with terror?). There is in reach of human speech an infinity of willed and dreamt supposition (an act of will is a dream in daylight). The conjunction *if* can alter, recompose, put in radical doubt, even negate the universe as we choose to perceive it. I have alluded to the insolubility, an insolubility which solicits rather than precludes metaphysical inquiry, of the question as to whether this unboundedness in language entails a preceding, generative infinitude in human 'thought' and imaginary representation. We do not know. We cannot, save metaphorically, ask in words of that which may lie before words. Though there is a sense, again metaphysically resistant and crucial, in which music does just that. What is evident is this: the formal and executive potential of words, of syntax, of scripts, to communicate – be it solely to oneself, be it via the unpunctuated stream of unvoiced address which constitutes consciousness – anything one wishes. Perhaps we do not attend to this fact because it becomes, when reflected upon, so overwhelming.

We can say any truth and any falsehood. We can affirm and negate in the same breath. We can construe material impossibility at will; in the Hegelian dialectic man 'falls up'. Thus language itself possesses and is possessed by the dynamics of fiction. To speak, either to oneself or to another, is in the most naked, rigorous sense of that unfathomable banality, to invent, to re-invent being and the world. Voiced truth is, ontologically

55

and logically, 'true fiction', where the etymology of fiction directs us immediately to that of 'making'. Language creates: by virtue of nomination, as in Adam's naming of all forms and presences; by virtue of adjectival qualification, without which there can be no conceptualization of good or evil; it creates by means of predication, of chosen remembrance (all 'history' is lodged in the grammar of the past tense). Above all else, language is the generator and messenger of and out of tomorrow. In root distinction from the leaf, from the animal, man alone can construct and parse the grammar of hope. He can speak, he can write about the morning light on the day after his funeral or about the ordered pace of the galaxies a billion light-years after the extinction of the planet. I believe that this capability to say and unsay all, to construct and deconstruct space and time, to beget and speak counter-factuals – 'if Napoleon had commanded in Vietnam' – makes man of man. More especially: of all evolutionary tools towards survival, it is the ability to use future tenses of the verb – when, how did the psyche acquire this monstrous and liberating power? – which I take to be foremost. Without it men and women would be no better than "falling stones" (Spinoza).

We cannot imagine being, and imagining is, immediately, a semantic move, without discursive openness, without the potentiality of questioning even death. Above the minimal vegetative plane, our lives depend on our capacity to speak hope, to entrust to if-clauses and futures our active dreams of change, of progress, of deliverance. To such dreams, the concept of resurrection, as it is central to both myth and religion, is a natural grammatical augment. And it may be, as I have sought to show elsewhere, that the fantastically wasteful prodigality of human tongues, the Babel enigma, points to a vital multiplication of mortal liberties. Each language speaks the world in its own ways. Each edifies worlds and counter-worlds in its own mode. The polyglot is a freer man.

But the unboundedness of discursive potentiality has its negative side. The unarrested infinity of conceivable propositions and statements entails the logic of nullity and of nihilism. In so far as they are language, this is to say intelligibly spoken or written, all affirmations, all 'proofs' of the existence or non-existence of God are unbarred to negation. In the city of words, equal legitimacy attaches to the conviction that the predication of God's existentiality lies at the very source of human speech and constitutes its final *dignitas*; and to the view of the logical positivists that such predication has the same status as nonsense rhymes. Grammatical postulates and demonstrations of God's existence – it is the relation of these postulates to our experience of formed meaning in the poetic which is the substance of this essay – can have validity only inside closed speech systems. It is for this imperative reason that ritual, liturgical, canonic codes of saying, as in prayer, in sacramental formulations and sacred or revealed texts, strive to close, to circumscribe word and world by means of taboo, of reiteration, of apocalyptic finitude. Each blasphemy, in turn, re-affirms the open indeterminacy of language.

Here resides the true sense in depth of the Judaic prohibition on the enunciation of the name or, more strictly speaking, of the Name of the Name, of God. Once spoken, this name passes into the contingent limitlessness of linguistic play, be it rhetorical, metaphoric or deconstructive. In natural and unbounded discourse God has no demonstrable lodging. This is the obstinate dilemma at the heart of Kant's cautionary metaphysics. Negative theology, this is to say the postulate of His non-being, is as legitimate in respect of word and proposition as is the dogma of His presence. Hence the symmetrical abyss within genuine faith and genuine denial; hence the potential anarchy of spirit on either side of the free spaces of utterance.

This same anarchy reaches into immanent existence, into the weave of words, voiced and unvoiced, written and erased, within which we conduct, within which we realize by means of speech, our everyday lives. The irreversibility of the word, once it has been said, haunts many cultures and sensibilities. As myths and fairy tales instruct us, the foolish wish, the careless promise (in German, 'to promise', *versprechen*, also signifies 'to stumble over words'), the erroneous verdict, the wasted password to Sesame, can neither be unspoken nor recalled. It may be that every utterance, every act of writing, obeys a principle of the conservation of energy as universal as is that in physics. Rabelais, a man word-possessed, fancied that all sentences spoken or set down since the inception of man were 'frozen', were preserved intact in some intermediate sphere, from which the heat of recollection, of need, of anguish, could melt and recall them. Expelled from silence, language does its irreparable work. Theseus cannot summon back (revoke in the literal, etymological sense) to his appalled lips and throat the unfounded but homicidal curse which he has pronounced on his son.

In words, as in particle physics, there is matter and anti-matter. There is construction and annihilation. Parents and children, men and women, when facing each other in exchange of speech, are at ultimate risk. One word can cripple a human relation, can do dirt on hope. The knives of saying cut deepest. Yet the identical instrument, lexical, syntactic, semantic, is that of revelation, of ecstasy, of the wonder of understanding that is communion. Reciprocally, speech that can articulate the ethics of Socrates, the parables of Christ, the master-building of being in Shakespeare or Hölderlin, can, by exactly the same virtue of unconstrained potentiality, blueprint and legislate the death camps and chronicle the torture chamber. The mountebank's virtuosity with words of a Hitler is anti-matter, it realizes a counter-*Logos* which conceptualizes and then enacts the deconstruction of the humane.

I have emphasized the enigmatic totality of possible discourse, the inherent power of all speech to make facticity of fact, the capacity of narrative to qualify all experience, however immediate, as fictive or illusory. I have stressed the enormity of licence within which man, the 'language-animal' as he is defined in both the Hebraic and the Greek vision, exercises the compulsion towards asking and towards meaning. More particularly, I have implied that any serious consideration of this licentious genius in language, that any serious grammatology and semantic mapping will conduct inquiry towards a valuation, positive or negative, of the theological. The chain of signs is infinite. It is one's perception of the nature and status of that infinity, either transcendent or, in the severest yet also most playful sense, meaningless, which will determine one's exercise of understanding and of judgement. Inhabiting language, bearing on language or the grammar of sense as it is instrumental in a painting, in an architectural design or musical composition, both the act of interpretation and that of assessment, hermeneutics and criticism, are inextricably enmeshed in the metaphysical and theological or anti-theological question of unbounded saying. "As I see it," writes Ben Nicholson in reference to the works of Georges de La Tour (these will be exemplary to my argument), "painting and religious experience are the same things, and what we are all searching for is the understanding and realization of infinity." Yes; but which infinity? Chaos, too, is boundless and free.

Because semantic means are unconstrained, anything can be said or written about any other semantic act, about any other construct or form of expressive signification. There is unbounded licence of possible statement about each and every text, painting, statue, piece of music and, in natural consequence, on each and every secondary or tertiary comment or explication arising from them. Even as nothing in our physiological equipment for articulation or in the lexicon and rules of speech prevents us from uttering the irreparable and the untrue, so there is no conceivable arrest, no internal or external prohibition – except in the wholly contingent sense of censorship or taboo – on the enunciation of any aesthetic proposition.

That Balzac could pronounce the novels of Ann Radcliffe to be superior to those of Stendhal (whom he admired), that Tolstoy could proclaim *King Lear* to be "beneath serious criticism", that Nietzsche could judge Bizet to be a finer musician than Wagner, are not bits of historical *curiosa*. These, and innumerable comparable acts of verbalized experience and judgement, be they positive, negative or undecided, are wholly legitimate products of the uncircumscribed nature of the semantic field and of the unmapped variousness of the human psyche. Nothing whatever – and, surely, there looms in this commonplace a vertigo – chokes our vocal cords, nothing gags our lips, nothing slides out of gear in lexicality or in syntax, to inhibit the assertion, voluminous, eloquent, repeated, if we so choose, that Mozart could not compose a passable tune or that Cézanne was a dauber.

The fact is, simply, this: inasmuch as the generation and communicative verbalization of all interpretations and value-judgements are of the order of language, all elucidation and criticism of literature, music and the arts must operate within the undecidability of unbounded sign-systems. Aesthetic perception knows no Archimedean point outside discourse. The root of all talk is talk.

Talk can neither be verified nor falsified in any rigorous sense. This is the open secret which hermeneutics and aesthetics, from Aristotle to Croce, have laboured to exorcize or to conceal from themselves and their clients. This ontological, which is to say both primordial and essential axiom (or platitude) of ineradicable undecidability needs, none the less, to be closely argued.

Verification and falsification are the indivisible faces of the same coin. How shall we go about refuting, demonstrating as false, Tolstoy's judgement of *King Lear*, a judgement which itself internalizes an explicative reading? The customary motion of rebuke has been psychological and biographical. We adduce in explanation and *apologia* for Leo Tolstoy's scandalous finding those personal circumstances, those storms of nerve and of spirit, those occult jealousies – the figure and fable of Lear had, in certain uncanny ways, prefigured the miseries of the ageing author of *War and Peace* – which provoked Tolstoy's judgement against Shakespeare. Such a diagnostic explanation may or may not be sound. It may or may not throw light on Tolstoy's extended polemic against the theatre, a polemic made the more opaque by his own powers as a dramatist. But no such analysis of motive can, either in logic or in substance, do anything whatever to disprove what Tolstoy says of the ethically repellent and technically infantile nature of Shakespeare's *King Lear*. Nietzsche's flight from Bayreuth, his poignant enchantment, sometimes ironic, with lighter, more melodious music such as that of *Carmen* and of his acolyte, Peter Gast, may indeed assist us in situating, in making rationally circumstantial, the excoriating attack on Wagner. But such placement has no probative force whatever in regard to the proof or disproof of the truth and truth-values of his critique.

We may deem the man or woman who declares Mozart's musical incompetence to be himself or herself deranged, trivially eccentric, self-advertising (most academic exegesis, most reviewing and professional criticism is just that), or tone-deaf. We may relegate to the limbo of derision those once-formidable literati, art and music critics, academicians who damned, say, Wordsworth, Keats and Shelley, who ruled that Impressionism was an ephemeral folly or who classified *Tristan und Isolde* as "a mawkish, entirely unmusical piece of hysterics certain to be quickly forgotten". But our derision, our more or less self-complimentary pleasure at such immemorial gaffes, as we now take them to be, has no bearing whatever on their intrinsic truth or falsehood.

The instruments of articulation, the sinews of syntactic and of semantic coherence, the reach of persuasive intelligibility in these 'inadmissible' propositions are of exactly the same status as in their antitheses. The outrage is made the more intractable by the source. No lover of *King Lear*, no eminent Shakespearian interpreter or critic, happens to be as profound, as sovereign a dweller in language and creation as was Tolstoy. What other critic of Stendhal matches the intimacy of insight native to Balzac? Nietzsche *contra* Wagner leaves perfect Wagnerites in the shade, in respect both of aural sensibility and expository brilliance. On either side of conviction, words are loosed upon words.

In practice, how do we proceed? By appealing, more or less overtly, to prevailing opinion, to the cultural, institutional consensus which has evolved across time. We count heads and we count years. Across millennia of Western reception, mimesis and thematic variation, across millennia of pedagogy, Homer and Virgil have been found exemplary. In our *civilitas*, Dante, Shakespeare, Goethe are of the core of literate recognition, inspiration and enjoyment (even if there is, on this third point, occasional room for irreverent doubt). When speaking Italian, English or German, when using that more diffuse general parlance which makes of these tongues the outward branchings of a Western post-classical and Christian community, we resort prodigally, and often unawares, to the more particular linguistic, formal font of the *Commedia*, of *Hamlet* or of *Faust*. Their elision from the alphabet of Western speech would beggar discourse.

The sculptures of Michelangelo, the interiors of Vermeer, Rembrandt's self-portraits or Cézanne's shaped meditations on earth and sky may, at first, have been provocations to myopia, to indifference or even to vehement distaste. Over centuries, they have established or are establishing themselves as the markers of our Western habitation of space, volume, colour and light. They are the referential "inscape" (Gerard Manley Hopkins's term) of our organized and informing sensations. Vermeer's treatments of fabric have schooled our fingertips.

There are, one has every reason to suppose, numerous men and women for whom an existence without serious music would be an inconsolable dreariness. Bach, Haydn, Mozart, Beethoven, the masters of song and of opera are to countless performers, however amateur, to countless listeners, tutelary presences. They are the custodians and initiators into felt intimations of open horizons, of well-springs of recuperation and self-surpassing for a constricted and worn humanity. I believe the modulation of music towards our apprehension and sufferance of death to be of the essence. Without the truths of music, what would be our deficit of spirit at the close of day?

Of these recognitions and needs, of their constantly recursive formulation and fulfilment, comes the canon. From the talismanic quickening of being which is ours when we experience, when we live the major text, the master-painting or sculpture, the necessary music, the syllabus is made. How else could there be a culture, a transmission of values? How else could interest and continued yield accrue on the investment in creation? Given the finiteness of personal existence and of institutional authority, there must be agreed economies. The inferior, the ephemeral must be set aside. A canon, a syllabus sifts and winnows so as to direct our time and resources of sensibility towards certified, plainly-lit excellence. The denier, the one who, out of bizarre iconoclasm or marginality, decries the high vintages in our culture, is a waster: of our limited receptive means, of the tested and accredited assets of grace.

Canons are not invariant. The precise counterpart to this problem is the deep, vexed matter of 'development' in Christian theology and history: how can there be re-valuations of, addenda to, that which has been originally revealed and given canonic ('classic') status? Within Western humanism, there are works of even the most manifest dimension which do not readily cross linguistic-cultural frontiers. The dramas of Racine, at once towering and local, are a troubling instance. Nor are the judgements of interpretative scholarship and general appraisal inflexible. A sometime classic can recede into purely historical and specialized notice. It is difficult, though by no means impossible, to believe that the *moralia* of Seneca, and the oratorical tragedies ascribed to him, will ever regain the pivotal place which they occupied in European literary and philosophic life from the early Middle Ages to Montaigne and the Enlightenment. Who, today, is truly conversant with the Italian heroic and mock-epic (Boiardo, Ariosto, Tasso) whose tonality and narrative ways are fundamental not only to the baroque, but to much of the Romantic movement? The early nineteenth century had no hesitation in assigning to Klopstock's *Messias* a place beside Dante and Milton. It knew little of Kleist and next to nothing of Büchner.

Correspondingly, what was once esoteric and hermetic can be recuperated for the general syllabus. Both Romanticism and modernity are peculiarly marked by this 'rite of passage' out of obscurity or critical and academic rejection into the established light. One thinks of Keats, of Rimbaud, of the Impressionists or the first Vienna School in music (Schoenberg, Berg, Webern). Deletion and rediscovery, zones of uncertain or conflicting assessment, are always present. Taste, itself an exceedingly elusive and complex category, is grounded in those very elements of language and of discursive qualification which are most personal, most 'idiolectic'. It is in examples of irreconcilable aesthetic disagreement, of non-communication between persuaded sensibilities, that we perceive most trenchantly the utter freedom and the gravitational pull towards privacy in all speech.

Nevertheless, the strength of the canonic is massive. It functions cumulatively within our earliest and our secondary schooling. It generates the concurrence of presentation in the world's museums and concert halls. There can hardly be a night on which compositions by Mozart or Beethoven are not being performed and heard at numerous sites on the planet. No museum, no gallery relegates its Rembrandt or its Watteau to the storeroom. Our codes of literate exchange, of inferred recognition, are pervaded, as is educated parlance itself, by the august implication and presence of the classic.

This ubiquity has grown with the application to the enterprise of culture of modern technologies of dissemination and of reproduction. The photograph, as Walter Benjamin saw, the record, the tape and cassette, more or less inexpensive modes of publishing and marketing literature (the paperback), have acted as agents of canonic concordance. The issue bristles with paradox and demands careful statement. Malraux was right when he proclaimed the new availability, via reproduction and easier world travel, of all art and music however remote in time or in space. Oceanic sculpture, Khmer reliefs, Eskimo carvings, early medieval polyphony, can enter our homes at the literal push of a button. At a deeper and contrary level, however, the economics of democratization and the market have underwritten the canon of the obvious. The 'great' painting is reproduced without end; there are up to thirty recordings of the same Beethoven or Tchaikovsky opus; 'classics' appear in manifold imprints.

The paradox deepens. Culturally, pedagogically, the packaging and high definition of agreed supremacy has produced a radical duplicity. The 'great books', the pre-eminent works of the masters of music and of the arts, are accessible and widely communicated as never before. Yet it is this accessibility and consensus which diminish the potential for immediate encounter with the aesthetic experience and for the absolute freedom without which such encounter remains spurious. I shall be seeking to define closely the two concepts of 'immediacy' and of 'freedom'. It may be that in no civilization preceding ours, save in hieratic Byzantium, has the domination of the canonized and heuristic past lain as heavily on the innovative aspirations of the present. Latest estimates tell us that of all 'classical' music performed publicly, recorded and broadcast in the West, nearly ninety per cent predates 1900.

In the later part of this essay, I want to ask whether this paradox of total availability in the textual and the aesthetic on the one hand, and of a narrowing consensus on the other, does not reflect a crisis of feeling, both psychological and metaphysical, in our condition of modernity.

Briefly, I would direct attention to a second paradoxality, or duplicity. The canonic is held to be the result of a dynamic, gradually congruent process of felt truth. Men and women of normal (normative) capacities of reception and response bear witness to a shared sense of excellence across time. Each generation testifies anew. Slowly but, in the final analysis, surely, a construct of common values and spiritual needs emerges. There are pockets of dissent, remnants of dubiety. But the general axis is clear.

Does this liberal, evolutionary model match reality?

The number of human beings who, at any given moment and in any defined society, care deeply about literature, music and the arts, for whom such caring comports a truly personal investment and opening of being, is small. Or to put it more accurately, where accuracy is of the essence: the ordinary museum visitor, the fitful reader of poetry, of exigent prose, the audience for classical and modernist music as these are performed, broadcast or recorded, participates in a rite of encounter and response which, after the period of secondary and, possibly, of tertiary education in which such encounter may have been assigned its cultural and social functions, belongs less to the sphere of commitment than it does to that of decorum. In numerous societies, moreover, even this participation enlists only the privileged. Given a free vote, the bulk of humankind will choose football, the soap opera or bingo over Aeschylus. To pretend otherwise, to edify programmes of high humane civilization as arising from improvements in mass education – such didactic projections are active in Jeffersonian or Arnoldian liberalism no less than in Marxism–Leninism – is cant. Those who, in actual fact, generate the syllabus, who recognize, elucidate and transmit the legacy of literacy in regard to textual, artistic and musical creation, have always been, are a handful.

Thus the very assumption of a maturing plurality, of a broadly based catholicity of perception and choice on which the liberal, consensual case for the determination and validation of values is founded, is largely spurious. The statistics of the diffusion of cultural products mask the intensely reductive, specialized status of the few who actually initiate and encode the dominant currents and criteria. All valuation, all 'canonization' (observe the persistent theological analogues) are of the politics of taste. These politics are, in essence, oligarchic.

I have tried to make two points. The ontologically linguistic, discursive substance of interpretations and value-judgements in aesthetics makes verification and falsification logically as well as pragmatically impossible. No proposition in poetics and aesthetics can, in any rigorous sense, be refuted. The absence of constraint resides in the heart of speech and in the cardinal relations of 'being human' to speech.

Secondly, I have argued that the attempt to attenuate or to evade altogether this abyss of freedom by invoking consensus, institutional and social, across the ages, by pointing to the majority votes cast for certain works and texts over the long centuries, carries neither formal nor evidential finality. Truth, if any such be postulated in respect of the aesthetic, cannot be either proved or disproved statistically. I have suggested, further, that neither historical nor sociological fact truly supports the model of interpretation and critical judgement via evolutionary accord. The canon is forged and perpetuated by the few. Thus Kant's postulate of a validation of just understanding and taste by means of the consensual mechanism of "subjective universality", of an orderly progress from the intuitive findings of an individual to the calm waters of the public and the canonic, is either wishful thinking or an empirical observation of the politics of taste in a more or less enlightened, meliorist community.

If these points are of substance, the resort to the concept of critical theory, of theoretical authority in reference to literature, music and the arts, demands a close look.

3

The word 'theory' has lost its birthright. At the source, it draws on meanings and connotations both secular and ritual. It tells of concentrated insight, of an act of contemplation focused patiently on its object. But it pertains also to the deed of witness performed by legates sent, in solemn embassy, to observe the oracles spoken or the rites performed at the sacred Attic games. A 'theorist' or 'theoretician' is one who is disciplined in observance, a term itself charged with a twofold significance of intellectual-sensory perception and religious or ritual conduct. The original force of vision, of attendant sight implicit in the word, is present in Sir Thomas Browne's: "I have true Theory of death when I contemplate a skull, or behold a skeleton with those vulgar imaginations it casts upon us." Thus theory is inhabited by truth when it contemplates its object unwaveringly and when, in the observant process of such contemplation, it beholds, it takes grasp of the often confused and contingent ('vulgar') images, associations, suggestions, possibly erroneous, to which the object gives rise. It is only in the later half of the sixteenth century that 'theory' and the 'theoretical' take on their modern guise. And it is not before the 1640s, it would seem, that a 'theorist' is one who devises and entertains speculative hypotheses.

Thereafter, the history of the word displays a characteristic duality and, indeed, degree of self-contradiction. With the inward shift and displacement of understanding into the ego, the font of theory becomes a subjective speculative impulse. Descartes, Newton construct, propose theories of atomic motion or celestial mechanics. These bear their name. At the same time, however, the validation of theory is located in the world outside, in the realm of the objective. The dynamics of theorizing are those of personal consciousness; but theory only becomes something more than private conjecture when it is tested and proved by corresponding facts, by the mirroring evidence of empirical reality.

It is this model of creative, ordering supposition and subsequent experimental verification or falsification, a model given its epistemological patent by Descartes, Kant and, in a more recent formulation, by Husserl, which has underwritten the planetary success of the pure ('theoretical') and the applied sciences. We owe to its triumph the central claim to rationality in our exact and natural sciences, in our technology.

For all its prestige and accomplishments, the Cartesian–Kantian paradigm has been under critical pressure. Not only by those who, like Heidegger and Shestov (one of the most unsettling, humanely-obsessed thinkers in our time), have questioned its often destructive consequences, who have seen in scientific theory and its pragmatic applications a misreading of man's place in the natural world. The pressures have arisen from within science itself. The nature and philosophic-psychological status of the relations between mathematical systems and the world which they seem to organize or reflect has become a ground for intense debate. The notion of 'indeterminacy' in respect of atomic and sub-atomic interactions has put in critical doubt the deterministic classical conditions of proof, of experimental verification. The principle of 'complementary' – and we are here in immediate pertinence to the question of aesthetic experience – has even wider implications: it argues that identical phenomena are susceptible of alternative theoretical explanations and alternative theory-bound descriptions. Together, indeterminacy and complementarity presume an interference by the observer, by the process of observation, with the phenomenal material. To look closely at the world is to alter it (as Fichte knew when he argued his rigorously logical case for absolute subjectivity in the 1790s).

These critical subversions of the positivist scheme of the experimental verification of theory are, as we shall see, of the utmost suggestion to aesthetics and to an understanding of understanding. In the practice of the sciences, they have proved only marginally troublesome. Physics, molecular biology, astrophysics proceed as if the Cartesian–Kantian contract between theory and trial (the 'falsifiability criterion' of Karl Popper) continued to be valid and universal. Evidentially, moreover, it would seem to be so, except at the extreme edges of cosmology or in the penumbra of the new physics of 'singularity'. Our nuclear physicists, our geneticists and engineers get on with their investigative hypotheses and applied work. They formulate and formalize (mathematically) into practice theories and counter-theories. They address these, with palpable yield, to the matter of the world. The abandonment of this concept of 'theory', of the presumption of reciprocity between theory and fact, would be regarded as a termination of reason.

The ultimate grounds of this contract remain enigmatic. Why it should be that the external world, in the naïve, obvious sense, should concur with the regularity-postulates, with the mathematical and rule-bound expectations of investigative rationalism, no one knows. Bacon's famous simile of nature being 'put to the question', being racked by man's interrogative imperiousness, and of nature giving satisfactory, productive answers, obtains. Descartes and Newton make appeal to a divine inception and guarantee. Such appeal is, in regard to meaning in the language and the arts, precisely the one I am seeking to elucidate. Einstein's was the conviction that a higher order, that a refusal of hazard, animates the cosmos. Such inferences may be empty of substance or purely psychological. But the triumph of their application is manifest. The history of modern science and technology demonstrates blindingly (consider our colonized planet) that mensuration, the *tempora spatiis mensura mundae* of Bacon, of Descartes and the aeroplane designer, works. Theory applies.

What I now want to show is that the extension of this imperial model to the interpretation and judgement of literature, music and the arts, is factitious. Here the concept of theory and the theoretical, in any responsible sense, is either a self-flattering delusion or a misappropriation from the domain of the sciences. It represents a basic confusion, an "error of categories" as it is called in classical logic and metaphysics. To invoke and put forward a 'theory of criticism', a 'theoretical poetics and hermeneutic' in reference to the signifying forms of the textual and the aesthetic, in anything but the most scrupulously avowed metaphorical or mimetic sense, is to 'translate', to 'be translated' in the suspect, profoundly comical mode in which Bottom is "translated" in *A Midsummer Night's Dream*. Shakespeare (and Goya) tell us of the consequence.

My argument will draw principally on literature and language. But it seeks extension to the phenomenology of intelligible and representative acts of form as a whole.

Writers, philosophers, psychologists, historians of culture and of sensibility have their manifold opinions as to the internal origins, functions and qualities of the poetic. These opinions, together with the debates and counter-proposals they engender, constitute a voluminous corpus of secondary discourse. Such discourse can be of an impressionistic, non-systematic tenor as in the notebooks of Paul Klee or the diaries of Kafka. It can be directed at the specific object of aesthetic experience, as in Lessing's *Dramaturgie* or the evaluative critiques and historical chronicles of Sainte-Beuve. It can, on the other hand, be of a highly abstract, universalizing mode as in Aristotle's *Poetics* or the aesthetics of Kant and of Burke. This millennial body of argued opinion, normative or pragmatic, prescriptive or descriptive or, almost invariably, both, accompanies, surrounds and gives a discursive context to, literature and the arts, somewhat as the ground-bass does in the onward motion of pre-classical harmony. Be it stringently analytic or lushly evocative, it is itself wholly contained within the life and limits of language.

In turn, this corpus of interpretative and critical utterance has its history, its developmental rhetoric, as do literature, painting and music itself. At certain moments, in French and Italian neo-classicism or in Russian Futurism, for example, the reciprocities, the dialogue between the primary and the secondary texts, between the poetic and the programmatic-critical articulations, will be of peculiar intimacy. Form seems to encode directly certain abstract and programmatic schemes. At other times, during the rise of Romanticism or of Impressionism, for example, the new aesthetics, as they are performative within the work of art or the manifesto, will be at polemic odds with, or altogether detached from, the prevailing interpretative and critical idiom. Interpretations, moreover, do not only have their history. In a very precise sense, they have their own cognitive record and linguistics. Thus the epistemological and semantic status of propositions about meaning and formal worth, about the intent and the merits or deficiencies of this or that poem, painting, musical composition are a perfectly legitimate and often fertile object of investigation (Kant, Schelling, Wittgenstein have substantive points to make about aesthetic discourse). Histories, both analytic and descriptive, of the vocabulary, of the semantic fields of literary, art and music criticism can be of obvious interest. Consider the shift in speech habits as between Samuel Johnson and Coleridge on Shakespeare, between Vasari and Longhi on medieval paintings.

In turn, literature and the arts can be subsumed under a more general scheme. They can, as in the Aristotelian and Thomist anatomies of the meaning of man, be classified as specific manifestations of the appetitive or intuitively mimetic intellect. Marxism incorporates the production and distribution of poetic and aesthetic forms into its inclusive scenario of historical-social determinism, of representational reflection and mercantile consumption. Freudian psychoanalysis, which is at this point the almost naïve heir to nineteenth-century scientism, sees in the aesthetic impulse and fulfilment a mechanism, more or less infantile, of sublimation. The daydreaming poet (Freud's typology) and the artist seek to sublimate, in an endeavour at once neurotic and therapeutic, or to attenuate and postpone the confrontation of the mature psyche with the 'reality principle'. These diverse incorporations of the hermeneutic and the evalu-ative practice within encompassing philosophic systems, within encompassing ideologies and edifices of social or psychological doctrine, are themselves susceptible of study and critique. We learn much from analysing Aristotle on Sophocles or Gilson on Dante.

But, again, the point is this: whatever their prepotent claims to abstract universality, whatever their *imitatio* of scientific theory and crucial testing, these constructs of supposition are precisely bound to the language-circle. They cannot transcend the medium of their own saying.

This saying constitutes neither *a theory of interpretation* nor *a theory of criticism*, the two being, as we have seen, inseparable. However abstract, the explicative and the judgmental discourse about the text, the statue, the symphony, do not empower us to invoke the concepts of 'theory', of the 'theoretical', as these are used, fundamentally, in the exact and the applied sciences (music being, evidently, the complex and intermediary case). Those who proclaim and apply to poetic works a 'theory of criticism', a 'theoretical hermeneutic' are, today, the masters of the academy and the exemplars in the high gossip of arts and letters. Indeed, they have clarioned "the triumph of the theoretical". They are, in truth, either deceiving themselves or purloining from the immense prestige and confidence of science and technology an instrument ontologically inapplicable to their own material. They would enclose water in a sieve.

Two indispensable criteria must be satisfied by theory: verifiability or falsifiability by means of experiment and predictive application. There are in art and poetics no crucial experiments, no litmus-paper tests. There can be no verifiable or falsifiable deductions entailing predictable consequences in the very concrete sense in which a scientific theory carries predictive force. One must be crystal clear on this.

The analytic paradigm of tragedy in Aristotle's *Poetics* is patterned on, it is not verified by, Sophocles' *Oedipus Rex*. The distinction is vital. It is not falsified by the intrusion of extraneous, of comical, of historical material into *Hamlet*. Nothing in Aristotle's blueprint, where formal analysis is so palpably preferential in its proceedings, could predict Büchner's *Wozzeck* and the deployment in tragic drama of inarticulate low life. Boileau's neo-classical canon of decorum and of the utmost economy of performative means finds heuristic illustration in the theatre of Racine. But *Phèdre* does not fault the executive prodigality and, at moments, tragi-comic fabric of *Macbeth*, and neither proves nor disproves Boileau's classification and ranking of aesthetic merit. Henry James's studies of the art of fiction are a penetrating exposition of his own choices in regard to the novel. They can neither predict nor invalidate Kafka's parables or the nocturnes in *Finnegans Wake*.

A second point, of no less import, follows. In aesthetic discourse, no interpretative-critical analysis, doctrine or programme is superseded, is erased, by any later construction. The Copernican theory did correct and supersede that of Ptolemy. The chemistry of Lavoisier makes untenable the earlier phlogiston theory. Aristotle on *mimesis* and *pathos* is not superseded by Lessing or by Bergson. The Surrealist manifestos of Breton do not cancel out Pope's *Essay on Criticism* though they may well be antithetical to it. The failure of classical and of neo-classical doctrines of literary language and genre to anticipate the evolution of the prose novel, a failure arrestingly repeated in Wordsworth's Preface to the *Lyrical Ballads* and in the literary theorizing of Coleridge, does not falsify what these same doctrines tell us of epic verse or the celebratory ode. A Kandinsky neither supersedes nor eradicates the axioms of representation implicit in all preceding aesthetic programmes save the strictly ornamental.

The two principles of indeterminacy and of complementarity, as stated in particle physics, are at the very heart of all interpretative and all critical proceedings and acts of speech in literature and the arts. However conventional, however imitative of its canonic forerunners, each and every literary text, each and every painting or sculpture, is a 'singularity'. It is a contingent phenomenality which could or could not have come into perceptible form. It is, doubtless, under certain semantic and material constraints (the 'endless sentence', the impossibility for Praxiteles to sculpt in aluminium). But it is not a predictable fact determined by theoretical postulates or entailed by logic. Though the poem or the picture or the sonata may, indeed, be classifiable within larger historical and formal orders, its "holiness", like that of the singular act of being and of presence, is, as Blake has it, "of the minute particular".

And because it is the product of an individual process of intellection, of reception, of enunciatory style, an aesthetic judgement, an aesthetic decipherment, will necessarily interfere with, will reorganize subjectively, the text, the work of art to which it addresses itself. There is an Aristotelian Oedipus, a Freudian Oedipus as there is a Sophoclean. The Balzac of Sainte-Beuve is not that of Georg Lukács. In what sense are Reynolds and Delacroix, Vasari and Ruskin looking at identical Italian masters? Let me urge the point. We do not say Smith's or Brown's second law of thermodynamics. We do say, and with every justification, 'Pope's *Iliad*'. The implied differentiation is of the essence.

What, then, are so-called 'theories of interpretation', 'theories of criticism'? What are these proud spectres which now not only haunt but dominate approved perceptions and responses to enacted form? Any answer has, I believe, to be hammered out with extreme care. And it calls for a certain circuitousness or probing. But the issue is capital.

4

In the main and across Western history, critical theories in respect of the aesthetic have been *descriptions*. These are, generally, after the fact. They communicate the technical instrumentalities, the formal, social or political aims, which the analyst or the critic find commendable both at large and in the particular work. This idealizing, normative description *post hoc* underwrites the systematic poetics and rhetoric of Aristotle as it does the candidly intuitive formulations of a poetic canon in Matthew Arnold's 'The Study of Poetry'. It is from an emotionally charged apprehension of the excellence of Shakespeare's and Wordsworth's lyric verse that Coleridge's *Biographia Literaria* draws both its prescriptive commendations and *desiderata*. What is today known as *Rezeptionstheorie* or 'Theory of Reception' is, in actual fact, a generalized description of what is, historically, taken to be the dynamics of interaction between texts and readers, of what are, historically again, thought to be the modifications of significance and emotional tenor which literature and the arts undergo during the course of their transmission and reception in different epochs and climates of response.

There have, indeed, been attempts to study experimentally and predictively the effects which a poem or different poems have on this or that reader or group of readers. There have been attempts to apply techniques of psychological testing and statistical notation to our perceptions of sense and of suggestion in texts and works of art. One recalls I. A. Richards's "protocols" and "laboratory situations". But be it in either literature or the arts, such approaches have proved barren. No psychological schematization, no distributive curve, carries experimental or predictive force. Theory and the theoretical, however mutable their own history, however opaque their own origins in the conjecturing sensibility of the individual Galileo or Newton, infer the quantifiable. The mathematicization of the observed and to be rescued phenomena is the aim and tool of respectable theory. It may be (though I find it difficult to credit) that theory and theoretical modes do have validity in those spheres of demographic, economic and social history which are susceptible of a certain, always problematical, degree of quantification. In general history and the 'social sciences' – a term which is itself something of an eager sleight of hand – their yield is puerile. Observe an historian or sociologist resorting to equations and you will, well-nigh invariably, witness a retreat from thought.

What looks to be certain is that the criteria and practices of quantification, of symbolic coding and formalization which are the life breath of the theoretical do not, cannot pertain to the interpretation and assessment of either literature or the arts.

Here, as in every other respect, the matter of music is the most taxing and elusive. We know, since the inception of Chinese cosmology and the pre-Socratics, of the kinship between music and mathematics. Within Western music mathematics is, certainly since Pythagoras and Plato, in central, if masked, motion, as in a dance (even where that dance is performed silently). Though it has not until now produced experimentally verifiable, let alone predictive insights – why should G-minor be 'the key of sadness'? – the analysis of music does dispose of quantifiable units, of relations and progressions algebraically expressible. The notion that there may be quantifiable, verifiable correlations between rhythm, pitch, timbre, harmonic resolutions or dissonance on the one hand and the quality of emotional response, of conceptual-emotional correspondent imagining on the other, is not, *a priori*, to be rejected. The number and mathematical progression of vibrations in a given 'tone colour' are functional, are 'relative' to our response, as those in a Vermeer tint or modulation of tints are not. The mathematics of musical structure and the neuro-physiology of our auditive organs may interact, may experimentally be shown to interact, in ways susceptible of being theorized. We already have theoretical-analytic access to musical forms in a sense inapplicable to a poem or a painting, to a statue or a novel. Being most metaphysical in its intonations, reaching deepest into the lit night of the psyche, music is also the most carnal, the most somatically traceable of signifying acts.

I ask again: what meaning can we attach to 'hermeneutic theory', to 'theories of criticism'? What is as dour a thinker as Lukács doing when he entitles an early, fascinating book: *The Theory of the Novel*?

In the great majority of instances we are, as I have noted, dealing with preferential or polemic selections and descriptions of a corpus of texts or art. The Aristotelian anatomy of drama, the Jamesian programme for prose fiction, praise certain texts and assign to others an inferior or extrinsic status. Often, a 'theorizing' gloss on literature or the arts is an argument on morality and on the enactment of morality in the domain of political conduct. In the aesthetics of Schiller, in the proclamations of 'touchstones', of the 'classical', of "the Great Tradition" by Arnold, T. S. Eliot and F. R. Leavis respectively, the real issues at stake are those of moral education and political values. The "serene life of the mind and the spirit" which Matthew Arnold pleads for, in regard to which he chooses his poetic readings, crystallizes an entire scheme and politics of power-relations within society. Lukács's encomia and anathema are those of a refined Marxism.

Far more challenging to the anti-theoretical case are the fairly recent claims put forward by semiotics, in reference to the aesthetic as a whole, and by linguistics in reference to the textuality of all literature.

These claims are, if one may simplify their evolution, based on the understanding, after Saussure, after the Moscow and Prague language-circles, of language itself as a play of formal difference, rule-constrained and subject to a very considerable measure of formal and statistical investigation. And if the relational, differential sign-system which the modern semiotician and linguist defines as 'language' is subject to linguistic laws, such, for example, as the vowel shift in Indo-Germanic phonetics, why then should texts not be susceptible of interpretative and of critical 'theorizing' in the proper sense of that term? Why should there not be verifiable and falsifiable readings as there are of quantifiable, rule-bound evidence in the exact and applied sciences?

The argument requires scrupulous notice.

Unquestioningly, there are exact, formally assertable and, therefore, theoretically treatable aspects of the systematic linguistic study of speech and of writing. There are formal means of classifying and transcribing prescriptively the structures of syntax. A given text, inasmuch as its components are phonemic, phonetic, grammatical and lexical in both a diachronic and synchronic regard, inasmuch as these components are organized in (more or less) rule-governed sequence, can be studied analytically and statistically. The speech or writing act can legitimately be viewed as an encoding whose performative elements are subject to formalization, and within certain limits, to systematic decipherment. In short, there are mathematical or meta-mathematical (logically formal) approaches to the building-blocks and constructs of textuality. Here a certain measure of theory is in order.

But what measure?

The absolutely decisive failing occurs when such approaches seek to formalize *meaning*, when they proceed upward from the phonetic, the lexical and the grammatic to the semantic and aesthetic. It is this progression which no analytic-linguistic technique, however systematic its trappings, however abstruse its aspirations, has ever taken convincingly. The endeavour to do so has been perennial. We find it in the more formal branches of the classical studies of eloquence, in the ancient taxonomies and manuals of rhetoric. It surfaces in the subtle grammatologies of the Scholastics. We meet with it again in the more philosophically innocent versions of nineteenth-century positivism or in the ultra-materialist claims, fashionable during the early successes of Leninism and of cognitive psychology, that signification would turn out to be a neuro-physiological, even chemical quantum.

None of these proposals persuades. No interpretative method has bridged the gap between linguistic analysis and linguistic theory properly defined on the one hand and the process of understanding on the other. No formalization or genetic description has related unequivocally or demonstrably the discrete phonetic-lexical-syntactic components of a sentence to the meaning, to the lives (the semantic whole) of that sentence.

The reason is intuitively self-evident; but very difficult to articulate plainly.

A sentence always means more. Even a single word, within the weave of incommensurable connotation, can, and usually does. The informing matrix or context of even a rudimentary, literal proposition – and just what does *literal* mean? – moves outward from specific utterance or notation in ever-widening concentric and overlapping circles. These comprise the individual, subconsciously quickened language habits and associative field-mappings of the particular speaker or writer. They incorporate, in densities inaccessible to systematic inventory, the history of the given and of neighbouring tongues. Social, regional, temporal, professional specificities are of the utmost relevance. As the ripples and shot-silk interference effects expand outward, they become of incommensurable inclusiveness and complexity. No formalization is of an order adequate to the semantic mass and motion of a culture, to the wealth of denotation, connotation, implicit reference, elision and tonal register which envelop saying what one means, meaning what one says or neither. There is a palpable sense in which one can see that the total explicative context, the total horizon of relevant values which surround the meaning of the meaning of any verbal or written utterance is that of the universe as human beings, who are beings of speech, inhabit it. Thus the equation of the *Tractatus*, between the limits of our language and the limits of our world, is almost a banality. It re-states the incommensurability of the semantic.

I would define literature (art, music) as *the maximalization of semantic incommensurability in respect of the formal means of expression*. Here an object, the description of whose formal components can be finite, demands and produces infinite response. Each formal unit in the poem, the phoneme, the word, the grammatical bonds or elisions, the metrical arrangement, the stylistic conventions which attach it to other poems in the historical set or family, is charged with a semantic potential of innovation and inexhaustibility. The manifold of possible meanings – and the category of the meaningful is too static when applied to the poetic – is the exponential product of all possible sense or non-sense worlds as these are construed, imaged, tested, indwelt through the interaction of two liberties: that of the text, in movement across time, and that of the receiver. The internalized energies of reciprocal communication and suggestion, the 'quantum jumps' in this encounter, are entirely beyond computational analysis, let alone predictability. There is no science of sense and no theory of meaning and effect, if these high designations are to be taken seriously. Hermeneutic and evaluative propositions are not, as logicians put it, candidates for truth-values.

Language is organic in a sense more than metaphoric or pictorial. No enumeration, no analytic ordering of the units of a sentence yields a corresponding sum of sense. To elucidate sense, we paraphrase and metaphrase, renewing the indeterminate sign-sequence. There is always, as Blake taught, "excess" of the signified beyond the signifier. In the poetic, this 'surplus value' is most evident. Does this mean, as Leavis ruled, that "linguistics has nothing to contribute to the understanding of literature"? By no means. An informed alertness to the phonetic, lexical, grammatical instrumentalities of a text both disciplines and enriches the quality of interpretative and critical response. Roman Jakobson's dictum is cardinal: to know the grammar of poetry, which is the sinew of its music of meaning, one must know and be responsive to the poetry of grammar. The finesse, the knowledge in respect of the history of words which inform William Empson's *Structure of Complex Words*, the receptivity towards the areas of interpenetration between the syntactic and the rhetorical in the readings of Kenneth Burke, produce insights of exceptional authority. No reader can ever know too much about the bone structure and nervous system of language. But these means of penetration are, always have been, a vital component of philology. It is their more novel claim to a scientific-theoretical status which invites scepticism. Within the philological, a mode of perception which I want to define as essential, the role of the linguistic instrument is assured.

The incapacity of a 'scientific' view and anatomy of language to tell us persuasively of the origins of human speech, of the utter centrality of language-acts within the humaneness of what is human, or to elucidate for us the experience we have of the poetic; the necessary insistence of the scientific view that such questions are either otiose or unanswerable – hence not to be asked – are of the very first importance. They suggest that the notion of language as a purely interrelational play of differences, and the notion of man's life in speech as one of diverse language-games with no imperative of reference except to the pragmatic, are radically inadequate. It is, I believe, precisely this inadequacy which solicits a revaluation of certain 'outmoded', non-systematic, counter-theoretical intuitions or, as I would want to put it, compulsions to conjecture. It is because Pindar and Augustine, Dante and Coleridge tell of language in ways consonant with our experience of consciousness and the poetic fact more immediately sensible than those of linguistic and logical positivism and 'game theory' that the inference of 'otherness', of the transcendent, still commends itself to attention, to provisionality, a word in which the tentative and the visionary are so finely meshed.

To summarize: are all theories of hermeneutics and 'intertextuality' – a characteristic piece of current jargon which signals the obvious truth that, in Western literature, most serious writing incorporates, cites, denies, refers to previous writing – a waste product? Surely not. As we have seen, major interpretative-critical responses, be they in Plato or in Samuel Johnson, in Lessing or in Matthew Arnold, collaborate with the primary text in a distinctively vital manner. Current hermeneutic and grammatological speculations can be witty and challenging. The new semiotics and the acrobatics of deconstruction have helped to reclaim for intelligence, have woken to excitement, much that lay inert and formulaic in the study of letters and the arts. Where they are aware of their own essential reductiveness (what is more reductive, more narrowing of the freedom of the incommensurable in open forms than a Marxist or a Freudian decipherment?), interpretative and critical types of commentary can be of evident value. Where they do not press factitious claims to theory and the theoretical and work clearly within their own secondary, subjective and intuitive nature – all three qualifiers being of the utmost bearing – explicative and evaluative 'meta-texts' are both necessary and fruitful.

But it is not as 'theories of meaning' or 'theories of judgement' that we should think of what is most suggestive in hermeneutic-critical discourse from Aristotle to the present. At their best, these encircling acts of argument are *narratives*. They recount, in more or less abstract, in more or less formally sequent and systematic guise, moments of meeting between intellection and created form, a meeting whose source, whose first leap to attention, is always intuitive. They are, if we will, *narratives of formal experience*. They tell stories of thought. Longinus on the 'sublime', Coleridge's *Biographia*, Ruskin's *Modern Painters*, Proust's *Contre Sainte-Beuve*, which he himself wrote as an incipient novel, Roland Barthes's reading of Balzac, Harold Bloom on Yeats, illustrate this narrative unfolding. We may also conceive of certain explicative techniques as dramatized myths or mythologies of intelligibility, as fables of understanding. There are vivid scenic and mythological elements in the aesthetic criticism of Diderot, in the music criticism of Adorno, in Derrida's *Glas* (with its poignantly old-fashioned *mise-en-scène* of Sophocles and of Hegel). Narratives and myths are poetic genres. They are not theories.

Faced with that which remains incommensurable and irreducible to either formal analysis or systematic paraphrase in the poetic, in music, in painting, the interpretative-critical impulse grows impatient. I would define the claim to theory in the humanities as impatience systematized. Out of Judaism grown impatient at the everlasting delay of the messianic came strange fruit. Today, this impatience has taken on extreme, nihilistic urgency. It questions the very concepts of meaning and of form. It queries the possibility of any significant relations between word and world. It exalts the myths of theory above the facts of creation. What needs to be seen clearly are the historical and psychological roots of this challenge. Again, the final stakes are theological.

5

Fundamental breaks in the history of human perception are very rare. If this were not so, we could not translate into our own frames of reference, however imperfectly, with however suspect a measure of appropriation, the imaginative and intellectual forms of the past. We cite archaic myths as somehow elemental to our own constellations of consciousness. Writing has stabilized assumptions of continuity. We re-cognize what we take to be the spirit of the past by the force of the present letter. Historians of thought, of social institutions, of the arts, constantly remind us that the epochal breaks in our textbooks and museums, the disjunctions between Medieval and Renaissance or between Enlightenment and Romanticism, are largely arbitrary. They segment constancies of a far more vital quality. Even where one senses a radical dissociation, moreover, such intuition is most difficult to demonstrate. The implicit agencies of feeling are so complex, our own engagement in the material of so selective and enmeshed a kind, that it is almost impossible to be confident of one's finding.

None the less, there are, at a depth and at manifold levels of causality which justify the genetic term, mutations. There are fault-lines – here the analogy is geological – that break open the preceding constructs of identification. We are, I believe, at present within a transformative, metamorphic process which began, rather abruptly, in Western Europe and Russia during the 1870s.

Inevitably, one must generalize. But the status of such generalization and the logic of reinsurance on which our propositions draw are among the legacies most sharply in question.

The dissemination of literacy from the ancient Mediterranean world determined not only the experienced and recorded intelligibility of our historical postulate of self and society. It generates, it informs, our religions, mythologies, philosophic inquiries, our literatures and our arts. Even the non-verbal arts in the West have, until very recently, made use of an essentially grammatical and presentationally logical scheme. Our laws, our social relations, are inseparable from verbalization and from functions of value intimately inwoven in discourse and syntax. For us, 'literacy' has carried a weight of implication, an extension far beyond any technical definition. Ours have been, above all else, civilizations and communities of the word; sentences found and inhabit our cities. In essence, our history, in so far as it is available to more than private remembrance, has been that of discourse, both internal and external. (There is a fascinating, perhaps decisive history yet to be written of the diverse rhetorics and levels of idiom which men and women have used when talking to themselves in the incessant stream of unvoiced but organized speech which underlies, which envelops, outward communication.) Thus there is a bleak sense in which only the deaf-mute are extraterritorial to the pulsebeat of our collective history.

In the Western sphere, the conceptualization of God was at the outset and during its history in action that of a speech-act, of a grammatical absolute manifest in the tautologies of God's self-definition. Only death is outside discourse, and that, 'strictly non-speaking', is its meaning so far as its meaning is accessible to us. It is solely in reference to death that the great ante-chamber of liturgical, theological, metaphysical and poetic simile or metaphor – that of 'return', 'resurrection', 'salvation', 'last sleep'

– leads *nowhere* (which does not signify that the journey is vain). In every other domain, the phenomenology of saying has been, since Sumer and the pre-Socratics, that of indispensable relation to the presence and otherness of being and of the world. Of that indispensability, the concept and metaphoric reach of the *Logos*, in religion, in philosophy, in poetics, in the invocation and debating of the law, has been centrally representative. In our beginning, in an entirely rational, concrete sense, lies the word or, more exactly, the sentence. The inception of critical thought, of a philosophic anthropology, is contained in the archaic Greek definition of man as 'a language-animal', as a being in whom the isolating privilege of speech (isolating in respect of the rest of organic nature) is definitional. It follows that history, where it is human history, is the history of meaning.

So much is commonplace.

Less often observed is the act, the tenor of *trust* which underlies, which literally underwrites the linguistic-discursive substance of our Western, Hebraic–Attic experience. Often unregarded, because so evidently resistant to formalization, is the core of trust within logic itself, where 'logic' is a *Logos*-derivative and construct.

There would be no history as we know it, no religion, metaphysics, politics or aesthetics as we have lived them, without an initial act of trust, of confiding, more fundamental, more axiomatic by far than any 'social contract' or covenant with the postulate of the divine. This instauration of trust, this entrance of man into the city of man, is that between word and world. Only in the light of that confiding can there be a history of meaning which is, by exact counterpart, a meaning of history. From Gilgamesh's song of mutinous sorrow over his fallen companion, from Anaximander's riddling dictum about the secret of equity in the cosmos and in the lawful lives of men almost (it is this 'almost' which I am trying to situate and define) to the present, the relationship between word and world, inner and outer, has been held 'in trust'. This is to say that it has been conceived of and existentially enacted as a relation of responsibility.

As noted before, this noun houses a primary notion of 'response', of answerability. To be responsible in respect of the primary motion of semantic trust is, in the full sense, to accept the obligation of response though, as I shall emphasize, in an almost paradoxical freedom. It is to answer to and to answer for. Responsible response, answering answerability make of the process of understanding a moral act. This is the source and intent of what I am trying to say.

Until that mutation of values which I want to analyse, *Logos* and cosmos met – though there were always provocations to 'slippage', to radical inadequacy in their meeting. But via the roots and branchings of syntax, which are those of nomination and of predication, the word was held to be in a large measure of correspondence to the objects of its inference and designation. Truth, in so far as it was deemed accessible to the limited means of mortal supposition, was answerability to the meaning of the world.

The covenant between word and object, the presumption that being is, to a workable degree, 'sayable', and that the raw material of existentiality has its analogue in the structure of narrative – we recount life, we recount life to ourselves – have been variously expressed. There are different stories of the story. In Adamic speech, the fit is perfect: all things are as Adam names them. Predication and essence coincide seamlessly. In Platonic idealism, to which the main Western metaphysics and epistemology have been satellite, the dialectical discourse, if critically and stringently pursued, will elevate the human intellect towards those archetypes of pure form of which words are, as it were, the transparency. The correspondence between articulate consciousness and the matter of our perceptions and intellection, a correspondence indispensable to the very possibilities of rational thought and of social modes, is postulated in Descartes's *Third Meditation*. How else, asks Descartes, could we inhabit reason? The self-realization of 'spirit' (*Geist*) in Hegel's *Phenomenology* is an Odyssey of consciousness, of human understanding and self-understanding via successive stages of conceptualization. This voyage is made in and through speech. What is meaningful in history is gathered into the dynamic, elucidative custody of the rational sentence.

Scepticism has queried the deed of semantic trust. Sceptic philosophies have ironized, have sought to negate altogether, the correspondence between human discourse and the 'reality' or correspondence of the world. A veil of illusion and unknowing cuts us off from any possible cognition let alone valid enunciation of objective truths and relations, even if the latter exist. Indeed, that veil is woven and rewoven by language, by the imprecisions, delusions, pluralities, untranslatabilities and falsehoods, deliberate or not, which are inevitably inherent in every act and moment of human verbalization. A fully consequent scepticism will make of language a primarily internalized, conventional shadow-system whose autistic rules and figurations have nothing verifiable to do with what is 'out there' (itself a childish, meaningless phrase). A qualified scepticism such as Montaigne's argues the prodigalities of error, of misprisions; it points to the innumerable gaps and rents in the language-net as the latter labours to capture, to bring home to sensory verification and to intelligibility the elusive quarry of existence.

At the level of rhetoric and poetics, the motif of semantic inadequacy is an ancient one. However artful, however inspired, the words of the poet, of the philosopher, will fall short of the numinous intensities of certain phenomena and states of felt being. The aura of certain settings in nature, of certain privacies of desire or of pain, resists communicative transfer into speech. The only just response to Helen's mystery of loveliness and to the surge of Eros in her step is not speech but silence. It is not, says Kafka, the song of the Sirens, but their silence which carries the true charge of illumination and of menace. Not even the purest tautologist (a lexicographer *in extremis*) has ever held the total sum of essence to be convertible into the currency of the word and the sentence.

But the decisive point has been this: until the crisis of the meaning of meaning which began in the late nineteenth century, even the most astringent scepticism, even the most subversive of anti-rhetorics, remained committed to language. It knew itself to be 'in trust' to language. Pyrrhonism, which is the classical font and paradigm of Western scepticism, does not question its own right, its own capacity, to put its case in the form of articulate, grammatically organized propositions. Montaigne and Hume are major stylists, thoroughly at home in the house of language. Nowhere do they evidence any genuine, hence consequent, doubt as to the legitimacy of the linguistic instrument when that instrument is being used to urge the dubieties, the limitations, the unexamined delusions which subvert man's discursive commerce with what he takes to be the facts.

The point needs to be stressed. Traditional scepticism, the poetic challenge to the 'sayability' of the world, are themselves language-acts and verbal constructs. They fully assume the access to intelligibility, to coherence (narrative), to the means of persuasion, of the lexical, the grammatical and the semantic instruments whereby they convey their doubts and negations. It is just this assumption which does authorize the otherwise shallow objection that no sceptic, Pyrrho or after, has ever been able to apply his abstentions and refutations to daily life. Inconsistent with itself inasmuch as it has sought expression, scepticism accepted the contract with language.

It is my belief that this contract is broken for the first time, in any thorough and consequent sense, in European, Central European and Russian culture and speculative consciousness during the decades from the 1870s to the 1930s. *It is this break of the covenant between word and world which constitutes one of the very few genuine revolutions of spirit in Western history and which defines modernity itself.*

The new fabric of our culture and of the means of meaning which are instrumental in this fabric – though it is precisely the possibility of any such definition which is at stake – can best be expressed by saying that our inward history, that the codes of perception and self-perception through which we situate our relations of intelligibility to others and to 'the world', have entered upon a second major phase. In shorthand: the first, which extended from the beginnings of recorded history and propositional utterance (in the pre-Socratics) to the later nine-teenth century, is that of the *Logos*, of the saying of being. The second phase is that which comes after. Crucial configurations and operative modes in our moral, philosophic, psychological condition, in our aesthetics, in the formative interactions between consciousness and the pre-conscious, in the relations between the economics of need and desire on the one hand and those of social constraint on the other, must now be understood as coming 'after the Word'. Of this posterity, the vulgarized shibboleth of the "death of God" is a seminal but only partial articulation.

The specific problems of value and interpretation, of text and answerability with which this essay is concerned derive directly from this break. Throughout, my question is: what is the status and meaning of meaning, of communicative form, in the time of the 'after-Word'? I define this time as that of the *epilogue* (again, the term houses *Logos*). I ask the question in the full realization of the fact that 'after-words' are also prefaces and new beginnings.

6

The causes in depth of such a revolution lie beyond our adequate understanding. The proud systems of the historicity of consciousness so characteristic of Romanticism, the attempts by Hegel, Schelling and Comte to discover and expound the laws of the development of human consciousness, now strike us as illusory. In close analogy to their literary counterparts, such as Joyce's *Ulysses* or Pound's *Cantos*, they represent a terminal lunge towards totality, towards a controlled in-gathering of all cultural-historical values and legacies. A peculiar sadness inhabits even their most magisterial, forward movements. It comes from an intimation of the nearing crisis, from a clairvoyance into twilight.

But if we cannot, confidently, determine the deep-lying forces which brought on the crisis of the word, we can, I believe, identify some of the actual moments and pronouncements, some of the attitudes and texts or works of art, at which, in which, the crisis became a fact of awareness. We can, I think, cite certain things said or unsaid irretrievably, in which Western consciousness, in respect of its literacy and commitment to an 'examined life' (the Socratic groundrule), moves house.

This move is first declared in Mallarmé's disjunction of language from external reference and in Rimbaud's deconstruction of the first person singular. These two proceedings, and all

that they entail, splinter the foundations of the Hebraic–Hellenic
–Cartesian edifice in which the *ratio* and psychology of the
Western communicative tradition had lodged. Compared to this
fragmentation, even the political revolutions and great wars in
modern European history are, I would venture, of the surface.

The word *rose* has neither stem nor leaf nor thorn. It is neither
pink nor red nor yellow. It exudes no odour. It is, *per se*, a wholly
arbitrary phonetic marker, an empty sign. Nothing whatever in
its (minimal) sonority, in its graphic appearance, in its phonemic
components, etymological history or grammatical functions, has
any correspondence whatever to what we believe or imagine to
be the object of its purely conventional reference. Of that object
'in itself', of its 'true' existence or essence, we can, as Kant has
taught us, know strictly nothing. *A fortiori*, the word *rose* cannot
instruct us. The organization of our senses, the structures which
generate intellection and expression are either beyond our
cognition or self-referring or both. Language is embedded in
these organizations and structures. There is no external Archimedean point to give it referential autonomy and authority. This
concept of language is, we have seen, inherent in scepticism. It
has adumbrations in certain elements of Renaissance linguistic
speculation. Saussure will give it canonic and systematic form.
But Mallarmé goes further, and his is the ontologically critical
step.

To ascribe to words a correspondence to 'things out there', to
see and use them as somehow representational of 'reality' in the
world, is not only a vulgar illusion. It makes of language a lie.
To use the word *rose* as if it was, in any way, like what we
conceive to be some botanical phenomenon, to ask of any word
that it stand in lieu of, as a surrogate for, the perfectly inaccessible
'truths' of substance, is to abuse and demean it. It is to encrust

language with falsehood ("impure" is Mallarmé's preferred epithet).

That which endows the word *rose*, that arbitrary assemblage of two vowels and two consonants, with its sole legitimacy and life force is, states Mallarmé, "*l'absence de toute rose*". Unless I am mistaken, we stand here at the precise source of philosophic and aesthetic modernity, at the breakpoint with the *Logos*-order as Western thought and feeling had known it since, at the least, the tautology spoken from the Burning Bush. We are here at the exact parting of the semantic ways which will lead, also, to modernity in the discourse of physics, to Heisenberg's postulate that "Relations are only speakable as images and parallels."

A *Logos*-order entails, as I want to show, a central supposition of 'real presence'. Mallarmé's repudiation of the covenant of reference, and his insistence that non-reference constitutes the true genius and purity of language, entail a central supposition of 'real absence'. Their consequence is in a rigorous philosophic-semantic sense (where both the philosophical and the semantic eventuality are in doubt) an ontological nihilism (such as Heidegger will explore in his exposition of 'Nothingness' or *Nichtigkeit*). Between the four arbitrary signs which make up – where 'make up' has its full fictive connotation – the verbal or graphic object *rose*, between the syntactic rules of the particular language-game in which this object has relational legitimacy (it relates to other verbal and graphic markers) and the putative flower, there is now a gap which is, strictly considered, infinite. The truth of the word is the absence of the world.

Long after the retraction of Ptolemaic, geocentric astronomy, our daily metaphors, our usages in ordinary discourse continue to be those of 'sunrise' and of 'sunset'. Long after the instauration of molecular chemistry and particle physics, we persist in imaging, in speaking of the tables and chairs around us as if they were solid bits of matter in an Aristotelian order. So it is in regard to Mallarmé's revolutionary epistemology and linguistics of 'real absence'. Everything in our speech habits protests against Mallarmé's finding.

But this, precisely, is his starting point. Used (misused) as some kind of representational grid or facsimile of 'the real', language has indeed withered to inert routine and cliché. Made to stand for inaccessible phenomenalities, words have been reduced to corrupt servitude. They are no longer fit for poets or rigorous thinkers (poetry being thought at its most rigorous). Only when we realize that what words refer to are other words, that any speech-act in reference to experience is always a 'saying in other words', can we return to a true freedom. It is within the language system alone that we possess liberties of construction and of deconstruction, of remembrance and of futurity, so boundless, so dynamic, so proper to the evident uniqueness of human thought and imagining that, in comparison, external reality, whatever that might or might not be, is little more than brute intractability and deprivation.

Thus the self-referential, self-regulating and transformative cosmos of discourse is neither like the world, nor unlike it (how would we know?). It is not, as neo-Platonism and Romanticism would have it, a luminous veil behind which we discern the lineaments of a higher, more beauteous and consoling order. We do not, via language, transcend the real towards the more real. Words neither say nor un-say the realm of matter, of contingent mundanity, of 'the other'. Language speaks itself or, as Heidegger, in direct reprise of Mallarmé, puts it, *"Die Sprache spricht"* (but just this, as we shall see, is Heidegger's initial step out of nihilism and towards a counter-Mallarméan ontology of presence).

Enfranchised from the servitude of representation, purged of the lies, imprecisions and utilitarian dross which this servitude has brought with it, the 'word-world' can, via poetry and the poetics of thought in philosophy, resume its magic, its formal and categorical infinity. *Pace* Adam, *lion* neither roars nor defecates. Freed from any representational obligations on behalf of these functions, the word *lion* can now enter the reticulative unboundedness of its lexical-grammatical universe. There it can 'become' – which does not, of course, mean that it 'is', that it 'stands for' – either the head of a chrysanthemum, as in Marianne Moore's famous simile, or a lineament of the Zodiac. In such metamorphic becoming and refusal of empirical correspondence, *lion* will interact with, will quicken into fresh life other words from which the flower or the star cluster are as wholly absent as is the tawny malodorous quadruped. Neither the poem nor the metaphysical system is made of 'ideas', of verbalized external data. They are made of words. Paintings are, insisted Degas, made of pigments and internally relational spaces. Music is made of conventionally organized sounds. It signifies only itself. And it is proportionately to the degree that it approaches the condition of music and the self-contained autonomy of the musical code that, for Mallarmé and modernism, language comes home to its numinous freedom, to its disinvestment from the inchoate, derelict fabric of the world.

Such total disinvestment can restore to words their magical energies, can wake within them the lost potential for benediction or anathema, for incantation and discovery (key terms in Mallarmé's heir, Valéry). Only so radical a breach of what was a philosophically mendacious and utilitarian contract can recuperate for human discourse the 'aura', the unlimited creativity of metaphor which is inherent in the origins of all speech.

Rimbaud's postulate is no less revolutionary but, on an

immediate level, easier to grasp. *"Je est un autre."* English bridles at exact transposition. 'I is another' ought, in order to render the lapidary, counter-syntactical intent of Rimbaud, to be modulated into: 'I is an/other.' But the thrust is clear. The ego is no longer itself. More precisely, it is no longer itself to itself, it is no longer available to integration. Rimbaud deconstructs the first person singular of all verbs; he subverts the classical domesticity of the 'I'. The provocation is deliberately, necessarily, anti-theological. As invariably in Rimbaud, the target is God. But this aim is no personal quirk or chance rhetoric. Any consequent deconstruction of the individuation of the human speaker or *persona* is, in the context of Western consciousness, a denial of the theological possibility and of the *Logos* concept which is pivotal to that possibility. *"Je est un autre"* is an uncompromising negation of the supreme tautology, of the grammatical act of grammatical self-definition in God's 'I am who I am.' Rimbaud's decomposition introduces into the broken vessel of the ego not only the 'other', the counter-persona of Gnostic and Manichean dualism, but a limitless plurality. Where Mallarmé alters the epistemology of 'real presence' (theologically grounded) into one of 'real absence', Rimbaud posits at the now vacant heart of consciousness the splintered images of other and momentary 'selves'. And he does so in ways and in contexts which render almost inescapable the intuition that these other selves are not some neutral or parallel alterity, but parodistic, nihilistic anti-matter, radically subversive of order and creation.

Note the compelling congruence of Mallarmé's and Rimbaud's proposals with the fundamental crises of method and of metaphor in modern science. The epistemology, the linguistics of 'real absence' congrue with the physics of 'black holes'. Rimbaud's pulverization of psychic cohesion into charged fragments of centrifugal and transient energy corresponds not only to the

99

modern evolution of particle physics but, more stringently, to speculations on anti-matter. Such reciprocities at the level of perception and of inquiry cannot, I think, be altogether fortuitous. We shall see, moreover, how in both the arts and the sciences principles of indeterminacy become pivotal. In each of these methodological and metaphoric affinities – method being metaphor made instrumental – we experience the tenor of thought and of feeling after the Word.

The semantics of absence and the physics of 'black holes' and of anti-matter would have been equally abhorrent to Descartes. Concomitantly, Rimbaud's deconstruction of the self denies both the formal logical construct and the vital enactment of the Cartesian *cogito*. By definition, these depend on the unity, both essential and existential, of the first person singular. Rimbaud's anarchic pluralism makes of the Cartesian proof of being and axiom of rational relations between consciousness and world an empty vaunt. Translated into Rimbaud's counter-syntax, the Cartesian postulate reads: 'I think (I feel), therefore I am not I.' It is the other(s) who spring out of the tenebrous rebellions of divided consciousness.

In the immediate context of this study, Rimbaud's axiom of dissociation is of the sharpest pertinence. It generates, it justifies the erosion and, in the most consequent version of the case, the abolition of the 'author'. Again, we observe the close overlap between a theological-metaphysical and an aesthetic-hermeneutic questioning. To both, the assertion or erasure of authorship (*auctoritas*) is fundamental. Where the 'I' is not 'I' but a Magellanic cloud of momentary energies always in process of fission, there can be no authorship in any single, stable sense. The maker's – the poet's, the painter's, the composer's – will and intentionality in regard to his work can have no fixed *locus*. It becomes a logical and a psychological fiction. It is a trick performed with the aid of mirrors, but of mirrors, as it were, in motion and reflecting the mask of the other. A *Logos*-aesthetic and hermeneutic is one of reference to authorship, to the potential of 'authority' contained within that word and concept. All *mimesis*, thematic variation, quotation, ascription of intended sense, derives from a postulate of creative presence. The deconstructions of semantic forms, the destabilizations of meaning, as we have known them during the past decades, derive from Rimbaud's dissolution of the self.

But so, as well – and this is rarely noted – does a denial of the aesthetic and cognitive process of reception in any classical sense. Where 'otherness' encounters 'otherness', where fragments collide in unstable spaces of reading, of pictorial vision, of acoustic experience, such encounter cannot entail answerability in any Cartesian or Kantian way. The deconstruction of the 'I' and of authorship separates the aesthetic from the ethical. Where is responsibility, where is responsible response to be located? This severance is emphatic in the arts and culture of Western modernism as it was in the autistic poetics of Mallarmé and in the aesthetics of self-destruction – itself a practice and ideal in certain movements in recent painting and sculpture – of Rimbaud.

The great currents of the 'after-Word', whose emergence into declared awareness I have, for purposes of visibility, located in Mallarmé and in Rimbaud, took different (though finally related) directions. I will cite briefly what seem to me to be the four principal revolutions of feeling and of argument. Inevitably, there is in such an exposition more than a touch of shorthand.

Even before Plato's *Cratylus* and Aristotle's treatise "On Understanding", philosophy and logic concern themselves with language. The two are strictly inseparable. But as it is expressed in linguistic philosophy and *Sprachphilosophie* ('philosophy of language') after Frege, Russell and Wittgenstein, this concern is of an altogether different order. Within the analytic and logical positivist investigations into meaning, into what it means for a sentence to mean and for this meaning to be understood, doubts, critiques, remodellings of the utmost radicalism and consequence surface. As human sentence-utterances are lifted out of their psychological and social context, out of their contingent historicity, out of pragmatic, intuitive introspections, as they are circumscribed for logical analysis and logical-symbolic formalization, they lose their classical innocence. There is a sense, more than allegoric, in which language, prior to modern analytic formalizations, with their distant antecedent in Leibniz, had remained Adamic and pre-lapsarian. Now the very concept and realizability of reference, nomination, predication, interdependence, both logical and grammatical, are put in question. The force of this questioning is, as I have pointed out, different in essence from even the most pointed scepticism as it is tested in previous philosophy. It is not what is said that is being queried: it is the nature, formal and substantive, of the ascription of meaning, of intelligible signification, to the act and medium of the saying. What conditions, if any, would enable the uttermost sceptic to believe that he can communicate to us his suspensions or refusals of belief?

In their most challenging form, the critique, the abrogation of the innocence of discourse stem from Wittgenstein's reflections on and against language. The close of the *Tractatus* diacritically situates outside speech, outside demonstrable conventions of intelligibility and falsification, the domains of religious, of moral, of aesthetic experience and response. In drastic *ethical* contrariety to the logical positivists, for whom such domains are of the order of non-sense, but in *technical* concurrence with them, Wittgenstein severely contracts the bounds of that which can meaningfully (in 'an adult code') be said. In the vision of the early Wittgenstein – and 'vision' is the least inaccurate term – the existential realm 'on the other side of language', the categories of felt being to which only silence (or music) give access, are neither fictitious nor trivial. On the contrary. They are, indeed, the most important, life-transforming categories conceivable to man (but how?). They define his humanity. In the closing motion of the *Tractatus*, which is unquestionably kindred to certain kinds of reticent mysticism, Wittgenstein intuits an antithesis to the Hebraic–Hellenic definition of man as one endowed with the imperative of speech, as one 'having to speak' in order to realize his humanity. For the *Tractatus*, the truly 'human' being, the man or woman most open to the solicitations of the ethical and the spiritual, is he who keeps silent before the essential (or whose right conduct, the precept which Wittgenstein adopts from Tolstoy, is his true mode of statement). The better part of humanity within us 'keeps its peace' (a telling idiom).

For their part, the *Philosophical Investigations* contain elements of and incitements towards a total doubt as to any 'natural' model of language. Interpreted strongly, a number of Wittgenstein's questions and thought-experiments invite the conclusion that no such thing as 'linguistic meaning' is ever demonstrable. There can, according to Saul Kripke's searching commentary

be no such thing as meaning anything by any word. Each new application we make is a leap in the dark; any present intention could be interpreted so as to accord with anything we may choose to do. So there can be neither accord nor conflict.

Read strictly, such propositions as 201 and 202 in the *Investigations* allow no escape from the logic of a complete erasure of intentionality and verifiable meaning inside language itself.

No 'truth conditions', no corresponding facts can be adduced as existing in the world so as to determine and stabilize linguistic significations from outside. The elucidation of the rules used in any particular language-game or speech-move is internal and self-referential. *Strictu sensu*, any utterance may turn out to be a semantic singularity, performed according to rules which suspend or supersede all previous contracts between lexical definition, grammatical form and putative content. It is not clear to me that Wittgenstein wanted his supposition to be extended to its nihilistic finality. Such extension is difficult to accord with a sensibility which transcribed as that which "could serve as my motto" Longfellow's stanza:

> In the elder days of art,
> Builders wrought with greater care
> Each minute and unseen part,
> For the Gods are everywhere.

But this is not the issue. What matters is the logically licit, consequential evolution and deployment of the argument, as Kripke summarizes it, in modernity, in the complex of the 'after-Word' as a whole.

Mallarmé breaks (*rupture* becomes a cardinal term) the covenant, the continuities between word and world. This move in turn generates the potential discontinuities between the word and previous or subsequent usages of the word as they are explored in the *Philosophical Investigations*. We are at sea, uncompassed.

The dividing line between modern *Sprachphilosophie* (Tarski, Wittgenstein, Frege, Quine, Kripke), between formal-logical inquiries into the possibility and nature of language on the one hand, and modern linguistics in the more restricted sense of the word on the other, is difficult to draw. Logician and linguist, epistemologist and grammarian, work in close mutual cognizance, certainly since Saussure. But linguistics is itself a signal presence in the revolution of spirit and deconstruction of the Logo-centric order which I am outlining. There is here an absorbing paradox.

Together with linguistic philosophy, modern linguistics, this is to say the systematic, often highly formalized study of lexical, syntactic and semantic codes, has placed language at the very centre of epistemology, of social anthropology, of cognitive psychology and poetics. At no previous stage in intellectual history has the methodical investigation of language enlisted a comparable range and pressure of intelligence. How, then, can one say that modern linguistics is one of the agencies in the subversion and dissemination of the *Logos*?

The answer is that the dominant systematic language models after Saussure, and the dominant techniques for the application of these models, are antinomian to philology, both in the patent sense of that term, and in the sense proclaimed in its etymology. It is the latter, the interactions between 'love' and 'word', which I am arguing and seeking to clarify throughout.

The modern sciences of language, with their fundamental shift from a referential to an internally-relational semantics, would eradicate the last vestiges of the heresy debated in the *Cratylus*. That heresy was still vital in the Romantic movement; it inhabits every poet; it is the matter of dreams. But to the modern linguist, it is nonsense. There is in words and sentences no pre-established affinity with objects, no mystery of consonance with the world. No *figura* of things, perceived or yet to be revealed, inheres in the (purely arbitrary) articulations of syntax. No phonetic sign, except at a rudimentary, strictly speaking pre-linguistic level of vocal imitation (onomatopoeia), has any substantive relation or contiguity to that which it is convention-ally and temporally held to designate. The linguistic marker is as 'coded' as the algebraic symbol. For Mallarmé also, for Rimbaud in his exploration of the colour and connotations of vowels, any assumption of external reference was spurious. But within the language-universe, words retained their palpable magic, their specific density and energy of invocation. Scientific linguistics, itself now a branch of a more general semiotics or science of 'sounds and markers', excludes such fantasies. Rule-governed, susceptible of formalization on the model of symbolic and mathematical logic, the arbitrary set of diacritical sounds and signs which we call and experience as human speech may or may not refer to 'be like', the actual phenomenology of the world, whatever so crass a nexus might be taken to signify. Such likeness or unlikeness is not the primary attribute and interest of discourse. As it is not the primary attribute and interest of Euclidean and of non-Euclidean geometries (none of which is 'truer' than any other) to confirm or to falsify what our uncertain senses and chance needs make of the spaces in which we conduct our largely unexamined lives.

This severance or distancing of speech from the empirical, from the historical, from the Cratylean bias which quickens all poetics, is reinforced by transformational-generative grammars. These postulate autonomous 'deep structures' (neuro-physio-logical?) underlying all utterance-forms, structures which are of an almost inconceivable order of abstraction and universality (philology insists on the holiness of the particular). It may be that the neuro-chemical encodings of speech possibilities and constraints in some manner reflect, are analogous to, the genetic alphabet and code itself. We know nothing of these levels worth knowing. What counts is the formal nature and rigorous internalization of the entire system, of the 'wiring'. The word is not learnt from, it is not an historical response to, the world.

Not all schools of post-Saussurian linguistics have relinquished the pragmatical, the historical-social context. Not all have turned away from what is called, almost pejoratively, 'natural language'. Nevertheless, the shift from a semantics of correspondence and of reference 'outward' has been drastic. The analytic and structural study of language 'after the Word' has been one of *ab-straction*. Language has been withdrawn, excised from the anarchic weave of empirical experience and untutored intuition (gently, Quine calls such intuition "blameless"). Severed from their transcendental and mytho-poetic claims, the language-acts of man have now been identified as units in a conventional algorithm. Crucially, this algorithm is only one among many in the semiotic spectrum. Among these, mathematics, symbolic logic or the analogue or digital codes of the computer, perform certain tasks more clearly, more economically and, perhaps, creatively than does language. Thus – and we return here to our initial paradox – linguistics after Saussure has simultaneously placed language at the centre of human phenomenology, and has made of this centre a 'formality'. "Erasure rules" are not an object of love.

A comparable dual, and in certain regards contradictory, impulse towards language is consequent on psychoanalysis.

No summary remarks can come anywhere near the scope and importance of this theme. Psychoanalysis is, *in toto*, a language art, a language *praxis*. There can be neither mute patients nor deaf analysts. Psychoanalysis is as immediate to word and syntax as mining is to the earth. The Freudian mapping of the individual psyche and of civilization, Freudian interpretation and the resulting therapy, depend wholly on the Hebraic–Hellenic postulate and legacy of discourse and of text. Human consciousness is 'scripted' and made intelligible by semantic decipherment. The psychoanalytic movement, as it arises out of a problematized Judaism in Central Europe on the eve of catastrophe, is itself a symptom of the larger crises of the word and of meaning as I am trying to delineate them. Psychoanalysis dramatizes, seeks to overcome rationally and therapeutically, the conflict between *auctoritas* and spontaneity, between pre-scription (the 'script prior to ourselves') and freedom, as this conflict becomes acute in the breakdown of *Logos*-values. Ineluct-ably embedded in language is the paternalism, the jealous, outworn authority of the speech system into which, unchoosing, we are born. We toil under the alienating weight of its rules, ordinances, precedents (those Mosaic tautologies and clichés of 'correction'). The Oedipus complex is at the same time biological-cultural and linguistic: our language inheritance is the father figure, the prepotent figure of speech, which threatens to devour the autonomy, the novelty, the immediacy to ourselves (the idiolect) towards which our feelings, thoughts and needs strive. The libidinal psyche labours towards anarchic and creative egotism of utterance. It would hammer out, often in and via dreams, a vocabulary, a grammar, an associative field, appro-priate wholly to itself and declaratory of its unrepeatable being (Mallarmé's "purity" of words unsoiled by the "usage of the tribe"). Thus, there is one sense, and a major one, in which the Freudian paradigm of the articulate psyche is poetic, is potentially self- and world-creating. Hence the constant Freu-dian resort to literature not only for exemplification, but what matters far more, for *proof*.

But by peeling away the onion-skin layers, the inauthentic accretions which smother the core of vital expressive need, psychoanalysis radically undermines the status of the word. Analyst and patient, as they descend the tenebrous spiral staircase of the bruised, stuttering self, hope to bring under-standing and a healing measure of acceptance – these, too, are verbal constructs – to bear on the incipience of the speech process, on the shadow-line where the pre- and the sub-conscious surge of the psyche must pass through the narrowing gates of inherited, public linguistic codes. This enforced passage (those Chomskyan 'constraints') both 'maketh man' and unmans him inasmuch as it deprives his intended meanings of their primal uniqueness, of their correspondence to his sole necessities and imaginings. Only dreams and madness and, partially, the translations of these 'primes' into great art and poetry, circumvent this passage. Thus a contradictory motion is implicit in the Freudian proposal (a proposal which I, personally, find no more and no less penetrative, ingenious and metaphorically suggestive than was the faith in demonology and exorcism during the sixteenth and seventeenth centuries of European history).

If this is, indeed, the dialectical part of psychoanalysis which relates to Mallarmé's quest for purgation – *katharsis* is therapy – the part which attaches to Rimbaud's deconstruction of the ego is even more obvious. The Freudian tripartite scenario of the psyche (itself so beautifully a simile of the cellarage, living quarters and memory-thronged attic in the bourgeois house), the Freudian postulate of a many-layered and only partially definable consciousness, are systematic elaborations of Rimbaud's dissociation of the ego from the other and others within its existential activity. When psychoanalysis decomposes intentionality, when it dissolves declared motive into an iceberg mass of hidden evasions, suppressions, fictions which mask the self and mask it from itself, it is developing Rimbaud's intuition and Nietzsche's rebellion against any naïve view of human discourse as a vehicle and transmitter of intended verities. The concept, the hermeneutic and therapeutic treatment of utterance and of text as a palimpsest of superposed possibilities, in which each cryptic level subverts that which lies above it and alters that which lies below, is crucial to the Freudian reading of the relations, always both true and false or true in their falsehood, between the word and the self. It is not only, in Rimbaud's sense, that the 'I' is another. The tongues spoken by the two (or more) parties may differ to the point of mutual incomprehension. Thus psychoanalytic interpretation does not define: it translates into other, momentary, translations.

The fourth major movement towards epilogue can, itself, be seen as inclusive of logical positivism and analytic linguistic philosophy, of linguistics after Saussure, and of psychoanalysis. Again, no concise outline can be adequate, and the comprehensive term does not translate readily. *Sprachkritik* implies, as in Kant, both senses of 'critique': the ideal and the practical. It signifies a fundamental critique of language in the light of an ideal state, but also a radical critique of its actuality. Pressed home on metaphysical, moral, political and aesthetic grounds, this language critique is the representative and, it may well be, pre-eminent spiritual and intellectual act of European, particularly of Central European, culture at the close of the nineteenth and in the first half of the twentieth centuries. Diverse but ubiquitous, this indictment of language has made naked our modernity.

Its programme and many of its ramifications in practice are set out in a now little-read yet seminal work: Fritz Mauthner's *Beiträge zu einer Kritik der Sprache*, whose first three parts appeared in the emblematic year 1899. The brief of these *Contributions to a Critique of Language* is fundamental. The uses of speech and writing current in modern Western societies are fatally infirm. The discourse which knits social institutions, that of legal codes, of political debate, of philosophic argument and literary construct, the leviathan rhetoric of the public media – all are rotten with lifeless clichés, with meaningless jargon, with intentional or unconscious falsehood. The contagion has spread to the nerve centres of private saying. In a dialectic of infectious reciprocity, the pathologies of public language, especially those of journalism, of fiction, of parliamentary rhetoric and international relations, further enfeeble and falsify the attempts of the private psyche to communicate verity and spontaneity. Language has, according to Mauthner, become both cause and symptom of the senility of the West as it lurches towards the silencing catastrophes of war and barbarism. Wittgenstein sought to conceal, by dismissive allusion, the force exercised upon his *Tractatus* by Mauthner's theses. In *c.* 1930, we find Beckett reading extracts from Mauthner to Joyce. The subterranean influence of the *Beiträge* seems to have been pervasive.

I have cited the demarcation of intelligible language from metaphysical, religious and aesthetic experience in the early Wittgenstein and throughout logical positivism. More sharply focused even is the despair in language (or 'of' language) in Hofmannsthal's famous *Letter of Lord Chandos*, written at the turn of the century. Here the imagined protagonist abandons his poetic vocation and, we are given to understand, all but the barest necessities of further speech. He has come to realize that human words and syntax, however exact, however honest in their intent, however suggestive in their metaphoric and presentational energy, fall derisively, desperately short of the resistant substance, of the existential matter of the world and of our inward lives. Speech can neither articulate the deeper truths of consciousness, nor can it convey the sensory, autonomous evidence of the flower, of the shaft of light, of the birdcall at dawning (it was this incapacity in which Mallarmé located the autistic sovereignty of the word). It is not only that language cannot reveal these things: it labours to do so, to draw nearer to them, falsify, corrupt that which silence (the coda to the

Tractatus), that which the unspeakable and unspeaking visitations of the freedom and mystery of being – Joyce's term is "epiphany", Walter Benjamin's is "aura" – may communicate to us in privileged moments. Such transcendental intuitions have sources deeper than language, and must, if they are to retain their truth-claims, remain undeclared.

Developed towards an explicitly theological-metaphysical category, the abstention from utterance of Hofmannsthal's Lord Chandos will culminate in the final cry of Schoenberg's Moses in *Moses und Aron*: "O Word, thou Word, which I lack" (or 'which is failing me'). Precisely because the golden-tongued Aron can discourse so eloquently on God and on man's fate, that same Aron allows the representational and symbolic lie of the Golden Calf and the loud riot of Israel's falsehood. To Moses the stutterer, no words are available with which to articulate the essential, the election to suffering that is history, and the real presence of God as it was signified to him in the tautology out of the Burning Bush. The fire there is the only true speech. Human saying lies.

Karl Kraus's language-satire, contemporaneous with Mauthner, with Wittgenstein, Hofmannsthal and Schoenberg, is the most telling we have. The version which will be offered by Orwell is, in certain respects, a more educative and efficacious one, but it lacks altogether Kraus's philosophic reach and apocalyptic poetry. Maniacally observant of the lexical and grammatical decay of literary, journalistic, political, legal discourse, exacerbated by the barbarities of the universities, Kraus set out to show how a civilization literally 'talks itself' to sordid death (Robert Lowell's "I've talked extinction to death"). His ear was so sharp that he caught in the bombast and *kitsch*, in the false lyricism and pseudo-scientific jargon, notably in medicine, of Viennese and Berlin-German prior to and between both World

Wars, the ground-bass of the nearing disaster. In Karl Kraus, *Sprachkritik* became utter clairvoyance. Listening to the Babel of the *bourse*, to the lies of pundits and politicians, Kraus said, even before 1914, that a time was fast nearing when, in the heartlands of high Western culture and literacy, men would make gloves of human skin.

Kraus read Kafka's sparse publications and sensed something of his genius. The veracity, the depth of Kafka's unhousedness in language hardly need emphasis. Kafka's work and sensibility are to our age what Dante's, what Shakespeare's were to theirs (W. H. Auden). But this work and sensibility regard language, as fathers speak it to their sons, as men speak it to the beloved, as they seek to express in and through language those "great winds which blow from under the earth", as scarcely admissible. What right has man to language when he can only articulate guilt, infirmity and falsehood? There is, in Kafka's prose, an Adamic transparency achieved by no other writer. The symbolic inventions, the thought, the intimations of encountered incident, pass through the necessity and economy of Kafka's German with the immediacy of light. But there is a sense in which they also pass through and well beyond their readers. Their possible confirmation, that which might be their truth-conditions, is located like the vanishing point in the arts of perspective. They lie somewhere in the space of the messianic, which is to say in a relationship between word and world so self-evident as to render speech and writing, such as we know them, superfluous.

If I construe Kafka's parables of the Law, of the silence of the Sirens, of the imperial messenger at all rightly (on this point confidence is misplaced), they tell us that it is the inevitable passage of language through our consciousness and acts, and the consequent 'bending of the light' by the lies, hypocrisies, cruelties, bureaucratic emptiness, with which their usage by fallen man infects words, which makes inconceivable or imperceptible (a worse contingency) the coming of the messianic. Silence is truer, though here too there is hopelessness.

In Canetti's *Auto-da-fé*, that great fiction by an authentic executor of Kafka's will and vision, words, ideograms, the immensities of script in the great library which is the sanctuary of language, perish in flame. Once again, human discourse, now self-consumed, returns to the Burning of the Bush.

Sprachkritik, which I take to be the central 'motor' and motion of spirit in our present condition, elucidates, accompanies a general retreat from the word. The sciences and technologies which govern twentieth-century Western civilization have become 'modern' and dominant in exact proportion to their mathematical formalization. Larger and larger domains of discovery, of scientific theory, of productive technological appliance have passed out of reach of verbal articulation and of alphabetic notation. Modern biology, genetics, physics, chemistry, modern engineering and cosmological conjectures can no longer be put forward or debated in non-mathematical language (Galileo was a great *writer*). What matters more: the atomic and sub-atomic states of experienced reality – this chair, this table, the dynamics of molecular biology, the spatio-temporal conditions of galactic structures and singularities, are accessible not to the literate, but only to the numerate. Common speech is Ptolemaic, alchemical, opaquely metaphoric in respect of the existential matter of the world as science and engineering perceive it.

The exponentially expanding use of computers, to which I have already alluded, has, to an unforeseen degree, deepened, accelerated and made ubiquitous the numerization of our professional, social and, before long, private lives. Computers

114

are far more than pragmatic tools. They initiate, they develop non-verbal methods and configurations of thought, of decision-making, even, one suspects, of aesthetic notice. Theirs is the new clerisy, a clerisy of the young and the very young who are, flexibly, pre- or counter-literate. Screens are not books; the 'narrative' of a formal algorithm is not that of discursive telling. Thus it is neither the *Logos* in any transcendent connotation, nor the secular, empirical systems of lexical-grammatical utterance and writing which are now the eminent carriers of speculative energy, of verifiable and applicable discoveries and information or, as French puts it more graphically, *informatique*. It is the algebraic function, the linear and non-linear equation, the binary code. At the heart of futurity lies the 'byte' and the number.

It is against this encompassing background of the crisis of the word, of the abrogations of meaning, that we can, I believe, grasp most cogently the negative semiotics, the impulses towards deconstruction, which have been so prominent in the philosophy of sense and in the arts of reading during these past decades. Theirs is the nihilistic logic and consequent extremity of the after-Word. They attach to the great revolution in the relations of word to world as does a satyr-play to the tragic, prophetic drama on which it immediately follows.

High comedy can be among the most searching and chal-lenging of forms. At their finest (in certain texts by Barthes, for instance), the new semiotics are a 'send-up' – Hegel's *Aufhebung* literalized – not only of their purported object, but of themselves. The deconstructive saturnalia, the carnival of dislocations, the masques of non-meaning need to be taken most seriously where they can be seen as a variant on merriment.

I do not propose to expound deconstruction (this has been done lucidly by others), nor to waste time on polemics, often internecine. Let me refer here, once and for all, to the often repulsive jargon, to the contrived obscurantism and specious pretensions to technicality which make the bulk of post-structuralist and deconstructive theory and practice, particularly among its academic epigones, unreadable. This abuse of philosophic-literary discourse, this brutalization of style, *are* symptomatic. They, also, tell of hatreds and bewilderments sprung of absence (the *Logos* being *in absentia*). But it is not the symptoms which are of the first importance. What I want to do is to clarify, with full awareness of the multiplicity of currents involved – the Marxist, the Freudian, the Heideggerian, the absurdist – the theological and metaphysical repudiations which lie at the heart of the entire deconstructive enterprise. It is in regard to the post-structuralist, deconstructive sense of the illegitimacy of the intelligible, as it was grounded in a transcendent dimension or category, that I want to consider this mutiny of theory (more exactly, of theory which is itself made suspect) against the authority of the poetic. Like Hegel's celebrated owl, it is at twilight, in the penumbra of epilogue, that this radical provocation has taken wing.

7

Deconstruction is theoretical. It is, to be precise, a meta-theory, which is to say a theoretical investigation and critique of all available theories of meaning and models of understanding. It aims to tease out the act of reading or of perceiving and interpreting the painting from the innocent or self-deluding carapace of discourse. It would externalize, hold up for demolition, the epistemological assumptions implicit or explicit in judgements of aesthetic value and in interpretations of sense. Being itself a fundamental critique of the very possibilities of meaningful reading and hermeneutics, ironizing (though this is true only among its most rigorous practitioners) its own means of negative assessment, deconstruction privileges the discomforts of the theoretical, of the fragmentary, above the unexamined rhetorical complacencies and comely formalities which inhabit traditional poetics.

At the same time, deconstruction queries the traditional hierarchical distinctions drawn between theory and act, between critique and so-called creation. It is not only that both are, both formally and substantively, made of language (art and music are more resistant to this equation). It is not only that the deconstructionist theoretician uses, generates words, grammatical sequences, which have the same intrinsic status (or lack of status) as those employed by the poet, playwright or novelist. It is that 'creation' and the communicative effects to which it aspires are themselves consciously or unconsciously – itself a simplistic, hierarchic verticality which needs to be ironized and clarified – shot through with theoretical presuppositions and self-justifications. There is no purity in *poiesis*. Metaphysical, political, social interests and concealments are at work throughout. Deconstruction will show that theory, visible or spectral, dynamic or vestigial, haunts the would-be innocence of immediacy.

It follows that, almost alone among cognitive-aesthetic movements and strategies of interpretation, deconstruction neither champions any body of past literature or art, nor does it act as vanguard or advocate for any contemporary or incipient school. The New Criticism and T. S. Eliot strove for the revaluation of Metaphysical poetry so as to underwrite, in turn, certain tactics of modernity. Aristotle was advocate for Sophocles. Deconstruction is, intentionally, marginal (a key trope) to all histories of taste and manifestos for innovation. It ascribes to no movement, either classical or Romantic, Symbolist or post-modern, any particular exemplarity or weight of promise. Such ascription would be a rhetorical gesture with political, ideological or diffusely opportunistic motives. Texts, works of art, merely transform other texts and other works of art in a reticulative and spiralling continuum across time. The informing fabric, common to all, is that of the medium and of available conventions. Individual poetic 'genius' or historical singularity are totemic notions, largely illusory.

This abstention from preference does not only have its methodological rationale. It is indicative of the larger condition which I am trying to delineate. The satyr-play comes *after*. The deconstructive move is ascetically impartial, indeed indifferent towards present and future invention and artifact (that the ascetic need not exclude the playful is shown by the deconstructive paintings of Klee or the music of Satie). Within the boundlessly substitutable weave of textuality, everything and nothing have already been said and thought to have been said definitively. Texts (pictures, statues, sonatas) are, as Barthes proclaims, formally limitless tissues of quotations drawn from innumerable clusters of preceding and surrounding cultures. There can be no reason to suppose that the rhetorical-grammatological operations – the language-games – which generate these conscious and unconscious patterns of quotation will alter because this or that aesthetic programme or cast of characters (the individual talent) alters. There is a sense in which new poems are merely older poems momentarily forgotten, where forgetting and recollection (more graphically and self-betrayingly, *re-collection*) are themselves tactical. At this exact juncture, and somewhat eerily, deconstruction echoes – but is not all argument echo? – certain Kabbalistic meditations according to which all speech and writing after the initial *Logos*-act, after the first and all-creating Word, are more or less superfluous reiteration or epilogue.

For deconstruction, however, there can be no foundational speech-act, no saying immune from un-saying. This is the crux.

Developing, radicalizing a Nietzschean intuition, deconstruction knows that there is in each and every assumption of a correspondence (however subject to sceptical and epistemological query) between word and world, in each and every previous rhetoric of direct or indirect communication and reciprocal intelligibility between speakers, between writers and readers, a declared or undeclared delusion, an innocence or political-aesthetic cunning. The ultimate basis of such delusion, innocence or cunning, its final validation, are theological. Where it is consequent, deconstruction rules that the very concept of *meaning-fulness*, of a congruence, even problematic, between the signifer and the signified, is theological or onto-theological (the Heideggerian term is rebarbative, but it elicits, like no other, the necessary unison between an epistemological and existential assumption of substantive meaning on the one hand, and a theological underwriting on the other). The archetypal paradigm of all affirmations of sense and of significant plenitude – the fullness of meaning in the word – is a *Logos*-model.

Derrida's formulation is beautifully incisive: "the intelligible face of the sign remains turned to the word and the face of God". A semantics, a poetics of correspondence, of decipherability and truth-values arrived at across time and consensus, are strictly inseparable from the postulate of theological-metaphysical transcendence. Thus the origin of the axiom of meaning and of the God-concept is a shared one. The semantic sign, where it is held to be meaningful, and divinity "have the same place and time of birth" (Derrida). They constitute the Hebraic–Hellenic copula on which our *Logos*-history and practice have been founded. "The age of the sign", says Derrida, "is essentially theological."

Pragmatically, that age may persist, as more or less pre-Galilean and pre-Einsteinian narratives and perceptions of the physical universe persist in our everyday lives. But deconstruction seeks to show the factitious laziness in such persistence. It seeks to exhibit the psychological evasions, the hidden political and didactic power-relations implicit in such persistence. Deconstruction is, therefore, not an alternative or parodistic epistemology of aesthetics and reception. It is, or ought to be, an uncompromising negation of meaning and of form as these are made the (fictitious) objects of both interpretative recognition and of consensual or 'objective' valuations. That which necessarily underwrites such recognitions and valuations is nothing more nor less than the myth, now glaringly untenable, of divine guarantee. In a time of epilogue and after-Word, a critique such as deconstruction *must* be formulated. It is Derrida's strength to have seen so plainly that the issue is neither linguistic-aesthetic nor philosophical in any traditional, debatable sense – where such tradition and debate incorporate, perpetuate the very ghosts which are to be exorcized. The issue is, quite simply, that of the meaning of meaning as it is re-insured by the postulate of the existence of God. "In the beginning was the Word." There was no such beginning, says deconstruction; only the play of sounds and markers amid the mutations of time.

When Barthes instructs us that a text is not a sequence of words, of syntactic forms enunciating, communicating any single, decidable meaning (or even constellation of meanings), his repudiation is put in unmistakable terms. No body of discourse has any "single theoretical meaning". None transmits the "message" of "an Author-God". There can be neither gospel in any authentic sense nor, it follows, gospel-truth. It may well be that our civilization, so representational in language habits and aesthetic shapes, could not have evolved had it not, unconsciously perhaps, violated the commandment which forbade the making of images, had it not, in ever-renewed *mimesis*, 'imaged' God and the world in the word. But it is precisely the purgative function of deconstruction to demonstrate this transgression. The breach, via *imitatio* and claims to meaningfulness, with the primal interdict on 'imaging' was, no doubt, comforting and even fertile (it did produce our culture). But it was a fundamentally transgressive illusion. We must now be honest and percipient enough to set the metamorphic *insignificance*, the arbitrariness of meaning, always open to deferral or to vacancy, against the fossilized authority of the *Logos*, of what deconstruction calls 'the logocentric order'.

The notion of vacancy needs careful definition. Western theology and the metaphysics, epistemology and aesthetics which have been its major footnotes, are 'logocentric'. This is to say that they axiomatize as fundamental and pre-eminent the concept of a 'presence'. It can be that of God (ultimately, it *must* be); of Platonic 'Ideas'; of Aristotelian and Thomist essence. It can be that of Cartesian self-consciousness; of Kant's transcendent logic or of Heidegger's 'Being'. It is to these pivots that the spokes of meaning finally lead. They insure its plenitude. That presence, theological, ontological or metaphysical, makes credible the assertion that there 'is something *in* what we say'.

Deconstruction challenges this presumption of insured content, of cognitive ballast. Deconstruction can be defined as an elaboration on Gertrude Stein's *boutade*: "there is no there there". The idolatry, the theological-philosophic animism in any pretence to meaning-fulness must be laid bare. Signs do not transport presences. Theirs is, in a sense consequent upon but far more radical even than Mallarmé's, *l'absence de toute rose*. It is precisely that absence which the sign stands for, which makes the sign functional. The instrumentalities of the sign are those, as Saussure taught, of 'difference': signs are made recognizable and significant by sole virtue of their differences, called 'diacritical', from other signs. 'Difference' is also the act of differing: signs are not 'like' the objects to which they refer or are conventionally taken to refer. Thirdly, it is 'deferral', that postponement of settled signification, that keeping in flickering motion which adjourns the illusion, the sterile fixity of definition. Itself an echo to Hegel's *Aufhebung* or 'sublation', Derrida's famous neologism, *la différance*, is crucial to the deconstructionist and post-structuralist counter-theology of absence. Even, as we will see, a 'negative theology' (one of God's felt absence) or Heidegger's enigmatic speculations on nothingness, fall short of the nihilism, the 'zeroing' (an important notion in Barthes) of the deconstructive.

Hence the role in deconstructionist arguments of spacings, lacunae, fissures and breaks. Again, the font is Mallarmé, whose typographical experiments with *les blancs* – the blanks on the page, the white abysses of silent nothingness between the lines – proved seminal to modernist literature, even as Malevich's blanks and 'white on white' were to prove seminal to modernist art. All these terms and devices are emblems of absence. They fissure, they disseminate any naïvely cosmological sense of a meaningful continuum, of a legible 'text of the world' in which grammar, logic and the implicit theorems of causality inherent in grammar and in logic provide safe bridges between word and object, between past and present, between speaker or writer and receiver. Deconstruction dances in front of the ancient Ark. This dance is at once playful, as is indeed that of Satyrs and, in its subtler practitioners (Paul De Man, for example), instinct with sadness. For the dancers know that the Ark is empty.

The deconstructive programme follows on this postulate of absence. Nothing, either in the lexical or grammatical elements or in the system which they constitute – the code, the rhetoric, the formal convention – can be finally determined. Meaning is, as Terry Eagleton puts it:

a kind of constant flickering of presence and absence together. Reading a text is more like tracing this process of constant flickering than it is like counting the beads on a necklace. There is also another sense in which we can never quite close our fists over meaning, which arises from the fact that language is a temporal process. When I read a sentence, the meaning of it is always somehow suspended, something deferred or still to come . . . and although the sentence may come to an end the process of language itself does not.

This description is itself a soft-edged view of the radical *aporia*, literally the 'unpassable path', which Derrida postulates in any search for meaning. Any truth-claim, philosophical, ethical, political, aesthetic and, above all (where the very use of 'above' should alert us to the unfounded pretences involved), theological, will always be dissolved by the textuality in which it inheres. This is to say that language inevitably undoes the figures of possible, momentary sense which emerge, like ephemeral and mendacious bubbles, from the process of articulation.

To invoke biographical, historical or cultural context, in order to make out and to stabilize possible meanings, is a naïve subterfuge. There can be no determination of texts by contexts. In deconstructive terms, the context, itself arrived at by verbal constructs, is boundless and indeterminate. There can be no 'saturation'. There is always more to be said, there is always something new or contradictory to be added. There is in every proposal of interpretative context a potential of infinite regress, as there is, by illuminating analogy, in any appeal to subconscious motivations or intentions. New specifications, new rules of the game – we recall Kripke on Wittgenstein – be they grammatological, semantic or historical, can always change or put in question our momentary ascriptions of meaning, "making the green one red".

The very term 'meaning' ought to be replaced by something like 'non-finite possibility' or 'tracings', as these are invoked both in Freud's pursuit of the spoors of the unconscious and in the physicist's image of the momentary passage of sub-atomic particles through the cloud-chamber.

It is, therefore, perfectly illusory to seek to distinguish between the undecidability – often conceded by earlier philosophic systems – of aesthetic judgements on the one hand, and the alleged decision-procedures available to the philologist, to the grammarian, to the epigrapher and textual critic, on the other. Interpretations of a text, a picture, a musical composition are no less open-ended, no less susceptible of rhetorical insinuation and dissolution, than are pronouncements of aesthetic valuation and preference. The linguist-grammarian, the iconographer, the musicologist, 'play with' their material exactly as does the common reader or the critic-reviewer. All belong to the species *Homo ludens.* We have far too long dreamt the lazy dreams of firm foundations, of theological-metaphysical guarantors and arbiters. The distant fathers (who never were) have left us. We must now face, indeed, disport ourselves within a universe of games in which semiotic structures and their messages are boundless, often discontinuous chains of differentiation and deferral.

This does *not* entail the abandonment of our reading and study of texts and forms, however precarious and self-ironizing the process. Meaning is, according to the deconstructionists, indeterminate but it is 'investigable' (Wittgenstein's rubric). Consider the mathematical and the natural sciences. They, too, are based on this very distinction. Sub-atomic physics, the cosmology of black holes, can move forward despite, indeed in the playful light of, the indeterminacy principle and the fact that our acts of observation 'dissolve' the observed phenomena. Mathematics and mathematical logic can get on with their high, pure games though they know that no axiomatic system can ever be proved to be fully coherent and consistent from within its own rules and postulates (Gödel's famous proof or, rather, disproof).

Further clauses ensue in the breach of contract with the old ghosts of meaning and meaning-fulness.

There can be no hierarchical cut between primary and secondary texts. Both belong equally to the totality of semiotic sequences or *écriture*. Both are scripts. The only difference between the poem and the commentary is one of rhetorical modes. In a profoundly nihilistic play on words – but how else can words be used? – the poem, the painting, the piece of music, but especially the literary text inasmuch as it is verbal, are seen as the *pre-text* to and for the commentary. Poems simply pre-figure, this is to say anticipate, their own misreadings. If there is in deconstruction any hint towards valuation, towards the choice of one text for commentary rather than another, it lies merely in the wealth, gamesomeness and ingenuity of the misreadings or emancipations which it occasions. From these occasions no finalities emerge, no 'arrests' of the infinite move-ment and choreography of significations (Valéry's dance-meta-phors lie close to hand). Appeals to bounded, let alone fixed, relations between sign and content, between the literal (what-ever, as Roman Jakobson used to ask of his students, that might be) and the figural, between representation and non-representation, as in abstract art, are sclerotic remnants of religion, of metaphysics, of gross positivism. They whisper of political ideology and authoritarian pedagogy. *All* readings are misreadings.

But it is just this that makes them creative. In the post-structuralist and deconstructive model, it is the reader who produces the text, the viewer who generates the painting. It is in the reader's free experience and ontologically irresponsible response that worthwhile games can be played with meaning. Aphoristically, Barthes equates the birth of the reader with the death of the author. Classical humanism, with its presumption of *auctoritas*, is replaced by a democracy of equivocation, by the hermeneutics of 'do it yourself'. Reading is perpetual re-invention. For the late-twentieth-century reader, says Borges, Joyce comes before Homer, and the *Odyssey* is a late commentary on *Ulysses*.

It follows that the genuine writer is a self-reader, a self-subverter of particular nerve and acuity. He tests his intuitions, his need to 're-write the rules', against the historically, formally available means of articulation (or of depiction or of musical composition). He knows that he cannot escape comprehensively the playful circularity in which the signified signifies in turn, and so *ad infinitum*. At best, and it is this which points to work that is worth successive misreadings, the 'great' writer or artist will communicate to his re-creators, present and future, the mythical impression that he has somehow overcome or, at least, weakened the constraints, the staleness of the established alphabets and codes. He will persuade us that he has, at some seminal link in the chain, opened approaches to new deferrals. He will, says Barthes, have instigated his reader "to unexpress the expressible".

In turn, the good reader or critic or explicator will aim to make the text *more* difficult to read. He will elicit the strategies which the author has employed, consciously or unconsciously; he will make visible the cunning, the *ruses*, the displacements between signs and emptiness inherent in the author's game and in the language with which, alone, that game can be played. What all parties must remember is this: the games of meaning cannot be won. No prize of transcendence, no surety, awaits even the most skilful, inspired player. He, in fact, will be the one in whom the displacements, the deferrals and self-subversions are sharpest. God the Father of meaning, in His authorial guise, is gone from the game: there is no longer any privileged judge, interpreter or explicator who can determine and communicate the truth, the true intent of the matter. These are effaced by language in motion even as it presents traces or simulacra of legibility. The Tablets of the Law, which Moses broke in a moment of deconstructive perception, cannot be re-assembled. If the letters are, indeed, of fire, how can they not consume themselves?

Today, we stand orphaned but free in the place of the *a-Logos*. The Greek word becomes Latin *surdus*. In English, a *surd* is an algebraic root which cannot be expressed in finite terms. It lies outside the commensurable and the decidable. Etymologically, 'surd' carries the earlier meaning 'voiceless'. At that point, it shades into the unspoken and the mute, into the opaque zone of 'surdity', which means 'deafness' and 'absurdity'. Each of these areas of definition and of connotation is pertinent. The deconstructions which I have summarized are those that challenge both intelligibility and vocation (the answering act). Play and silence draw near to each other. As they do in the music of Cage.

8

There are grounds for rebuttal. I have already alluded to the self-serving jargon which infects all but the (rare) best of post-structuralist and deconstructive rhetoric. One can also advert to the feebleness of the actual counter-readings and 'dissemi-nations' offered by the deconstructionists. When the text or sign-experience is to be (de-)faced and de-mythologized, the results are, again with some exceptions, of a portentous banality. Ambiguities, self-contradictions, breaches and elisions of auth-orial intentionality, polysemic indeterminacies, long observed and even decomposed by previous readers, are given the burnish of discovery. In regard to poetry and prose in the Anglo-American tradition, nothing in post-structuralist and decon-structive readings surpasses the playful, but linguistically and historically informed exercises of William Empson, most especially in his *Structure of Complex Words*, or the philological but politically-lit penetration of Kenneth Burke's studies in rhetoric, motive and grammatology. Even where it is manipu-lated by major talents, deconstruction tends to bear either on marginal texts (Sade, Lautréamont) or on secondary work by a great writer (Barthes on Balzac's *Sarrazine*). The classics of deconstruction, in Derrida or Paul De Man, are 'misreadings' not of literature but of philosophy; they address themselves to philosophical linguistics and the theory of language. The masks they seek to strip off are those worn by Plato, by Hegel, by Rousseau, by Nietzsche or Saussure. Deconstruction has nothing to tell us of Aeschylus or Dante, of Shakespeare or Tolstoy.

But however cogent, these objections touch only on contin-gency. Other important movements of argument and specu-lative rebellion have fallen into the busy hands of mandarin mediocrity and preciousness. In principle, the low quality of deconstructive work being turned out by academic mills cannot be held to invalidate the case itself or its potential. Some successor to Derrida may share not only the master's epistemological *élan*, erudition and metaphysical wit – a very rare gift – but could invest these in a truly literary sensibility, in a feeling for language and form, however wary. One cannot, in principle, exclude the possibility that a Roland Barthes yet to come will address his supple playfulness, his licentious dubieties to, say, David's song over Jonathan or the dialogue between Ivan and Alyosha Karamazov.

No: in order to be telling – which is itself an idiom all too susceptible of deconstruction – a critique of the new a-semantics and grammatology must seek out some central philosophic ground.

The deconstructive discourse is *itself* rhetorical, referential and altogether generated and governed by normal modes of causality, of logic and of sequence. The deconstructive denial of 'logocentrism' is expounded in wholly logocentric terms. 'Metacriticism' is criticism still, often of the most evidently discursive and persuasive kind. To some degree, symbolic logic has been able to develop formal presentations of so abstract and generalized a type that they can be used to test, to deconstruct other formal languages from, as it were, outside. No such extraterritoriality is available to post-structuralist and deconstructive practitioners. They have invented no new speech, no immaculate conceptualizations. The central dogma, according to which all readings are misreadings and the sign has no underwritten intelligibility, has precisely the same paradoxical, self-denying status as the celebrated *aporia* whereby a Cretan declares all Cretans to be liars. Immured within natural language, deconstructive propositions are self-falsifying.

But deconstruction can live very well with this impasse. To be self-dissolving or 'sublating' (Hegel is an invaluable ancestor), to entertain persistent illusions of autistic reference – these are infirmities wholly to its purpose. The impossibilities of coherence inside the deconstructive 'anti-text', the incompatibilities between what the text is effacing and the norms of logic and of causality to which it must resort in the very process of becoming illegible, are grist to deconstructive mills. The hermeneutic circle, the celebrated inconsistency whereby we decipher the whole by its parts and the parts by what we have taken to be the whole, is the very arena for the deconstructive game.

An analogous invulnerability shields the deconstructive appeal to 'absence'. It can put into play the patent objection that inferences of absence are disguisedly substantive, that the excluded re-enters by the back door. For deconstruction, the conventionally determined and deterministic tenor of all textuality, of all aesthetic formalization, excludes any demonstrable 'presentness of presence'. It is only by means of indirection, such as metaphor, tropes, rhetorical figures and polysemic uses of discourse, that even the most classical of writers or artists can adumbrate that which he is 'really' trying to tell us. It is of the fundamental nature of sign-systems that the fictions of meaning-fulness can be intimated solely from what 'is not there'. Again, one protests: are such elisions and indirections not, *per se*, evidence of authorial intentionality? Surely, the point about masks is that there are faces underneath. Does deconstruction not lead us right back to inherited practices of readings in depth, of decoding, be they those of religious exegesis, of traditional hermeneutics or of psychoanalytic unravelling? But it is precisely the mechanism of infinite regress, of ultimate undecidability in all such strategies which deconstruction points to. It is precisely the arbitrary – ideological, dogmatic, pedagogical, opportunistic

– uses of terminality, of end-stopping, which we invoke in our deep readings and elicitations of sense that the deconstructionist holds up for exposure. For him any criterion which aims to demarcate the bounds of permissible definition and relevance, which would set boundaries to what could conceivably have been meant or not meant by a semiotic act, is itself nothing but a further rhetorical move. The notions of meaning are always transgressive. New masks grow beneath the skin. Or to advert to a key notion in hermeneutics (as set out, for example, by Dilthey and by Gadamer): to accord the 'horizon' of the possible meanings of a text with the 'horizons' of the reader's individual consciousness and cultural-historical experience yields no proof. It is itself only a contingent device.

More suspect, it seems to me, is the lack within post-structuralist and deconstructive proposals of any psychology or "grammar of motive" (this latter phrase is Kenneth Burke's). Given the postulate of insignificance and progressive cancellation or erasure, why should writers bother to write and readers to misread? Is the whole affair a mere self-deception?

Roland Barthes's concept of *jouissance*, of the lightly orgasmic effects produced by the eroticization of the discursive process and of its reception, is one possible answer. Derrida's more covert resort to language-games is another. Man is not, as he is for any theologically or naturalistically grounded view, a 'speech animal' first and foremost. He is *Homo ludens*, a 'playing animal' (where both these fundamental configurations are interactive is in the anthropology and poetics of Aristotle). Play is the ultimate well-spring of un-saying.

I do not find this conjecture persuasive. But deconstruction will argue that the invocation of and quest for motive are themselves rhetorical scenarios, that they lay claim to exactly those transcendent guarantees of significance and finality which they would demonstrate. Historically, moreover, it must be admitted that psychological explanations of the creative impulse and informing act have long been the weak point in epistemology, in aesthetic theory and in the psychology of literature and the arts (Freud regarded the problem of satisfactory aetiological explanation as insoluble).

On its own terms and planes of argument, terms by no means trivial if only in respect of their bracing acceptance of ephemerality and self-dissolution, the challenge of deconstruction does seem to me irrefutable. It embodies, it ironizes into eloquence, the underlying nihilistic findings of literacy, of understanding or rather in-comprehension, as these *must* be stated and faced in the time of epilogue.

The abrogation of the contract between word and world, the decomposition of the self as we observed them in Mallarmé and Rimbaud (Baudelaire is also a source), found a logical deployment in Nietzsche's subversion of 'truth' and of 'truth-telling' and in Freud's critique of intentionality. Deconstruction draws the consequence. Without having either to affirm or to deny the "death of God" – such affirmation or denial being merely oratorical gestures on behalf of a vacant simile – deconstruction teaches us that where there is no "face of God" for the semantic marker to turn to, there can be no transcendent or decidable intelligibility. The break with the postulate of the sacred is the break with any stable, potentially ascertainable meaning of meaning. Where the theologically and metaphysically posited principle of a continuous individuality, of a cognitively coherent and ethically responsible ego is dissolved (Husserl's phenomenology being the heroic but doomed rearguard action in defence of this principle), there can be neither Kant's "subjective universality", nor that belief in shared truth-seeking which, from Plato to the present, from the *Phaedrus* to now, had underwritten the ideals of religion, of humanism and of communication. It is this very impossibility that defines modernism.

Thus the seductive force of the deconstructive semiotics of the 'after-Word' is that of a rigorously consequent nihilism or nullity (*le degré zéro*).

The enigma of nothingness haunts the inception of cosmological and philosophical thought in the Western tradition. "Why is there not nothing?" is Leibniz's question. The void and the abyss are eschatological concepts throughout religious mysticism and the theological speculations which, as in Pascal, have their mystical source. But it is only in recent philosophy, in Heidegger's *Nichtigkeit*, in Sartre's *le néant*, a variation on Heidegger, that the concept of absolute zero becomes almost obsessive. Whereas in common grammar, in the logic which that grammar articulates, the negation of negation generates a positive – this is Hegel's crucial dialectical move – it now produces a final nothingness, a midnight of absence. Of this consequent annihilation, deconstruction is the spectral trace.

I do not, therefore, believe that an answer to its challenge, to the negating epistemology of the surd, of the *a-logical* and annulment of the *Logos*, can be found, if it can be found at all, within linguistic or literary theory. I do not believe that "the dismantled fortress of consciousness" (Paul Ricoeur) can be restored or made stormproof by replacing this or that fallen brick. Appeals, however 'blameless' and commonsensical, to the pragmatic, to the history and daily volume of intelligibility, of mundane reference and interpretative consensus, which do continue to 'do the job' in the Platonic–Augustinian accommodations of our ordinary lives, will not yield an adequate reply. Or, more exactly, for them to do so must, I think, require of us a readiness to envisage, literally to look upon the face of, foundations beyond the empirical. We must ask of ourselves and of our culture whether a secular, in essence positivist, model of understanding and of the experience of meaningful form (the aesthetic) is tenable in the light or, if you will, in the dark of the nihilistic alternative. I want to ask whether a hermeneutics and a reflex of valuation – the encounter with meaning in the verbal sign, in the painting, in the musical composition, and the assessment of the quality of such meaning in respect of form – can be made intelligible, can be made answerable to the existential facts, if they do not imply, if they do not contain, a postulate of transcendence.

As I indicated cursorily, such a postulate is often hidden, it is often left undeclared or exploited metaphorically and without consequence, in most of modern interpretative and critical practice. What would happen if we had to pay our debts towards theology and the metaphysics of presence? What if the loans of belief in transcendence, made to us since Plato and Augustine in reference to signifying form, were called in? What if we had to make explicit and concrete the assumption that all serious art and literature, and not only music to which Nietzsche applies the term, is an *opus metaphysicum*?

There is a distinct possibility that these questions no longer admit of an adult, let alone consoling, answer. They may be mere flourishes of nostalgia and pathos. The cruellest of paradoxes in deconstruction is this: there was no 'place to start', but there is, in regard to our innocent, factitious, opportunistic habitation in meaning, a place at which to end. What seems clear is that the challenge cannot be evaded. The reader (the misreader) at our shoulder can be either a Roland Barthes or a Karl Barth. For the current masters of emptiness, the stakes are indeed those of a game. That is where we differ.

III   PRESENCES

1

There is language, there is art, because there is 'the other'. We do address ourselves in constant soliloquy. But the medium of that soliloquy is that of public speech – foreshortened, perhaps made private and cryptic through covert reference and association, but grounded, nevertheless, and to the uncertain verge of consciousness, in an inherited, historically and socially determined vocabulary and grammar. Autistic inventions, solipsistic artefacts, are conceivable. The notion of a poet writing verse in a private tongue or of destroying what he has written, of a painter refusing to show any canvas to an eye other than his own, of a composer 'performing' his score in mute, purely inward audition, is conceivable. It figures in Gothic tales of isolation. And we do have record of masters who have hidden or laid waste their productions (Gogol burns the second half of *Dead Souls*). But they have done so precisely under pressure of the other's intrusion. It is because the claims of the other's presence reach so deeply into the final precincts of aloneness that a creator may, in circumstances of extremity, seek to guard for himself or for willed oblivion what are, ineluctably, acts of communication and trials of encounter.

Why there should be the other and our relations to that otherness, be they theological, moral, social, erotic, be they those of intimate participation or irreconcilable difference, is a mystery both harsh and consoling. Goethe's question, "How can I be when there is another?", Nietzsche's, "How can I exist if God does?", stand unanswered. The desire for absolute singularity cannot be ruled out. But neither can the dread of solitude. The rapture of Narcissus is, tautologically, that of suicide. And Narcissus has no need of art. In him, utterance, fantastication, the making of an image, come home, fatally, to the closed self. On the edge of that perfect adequacy of selfhood, Descartes, in his third *Meditation*, calls upon the imperative likelihood of God in order to escape from the finality of aloneness.

It is out of the fact of confrontation, of affront in the literal sense of the term, that we communicate in words, that we externalize shapes and colours, that we emit organized sounds in the forms of music. "Mute inglorious Miltons" are distinctly possible in the concrete sense in which personal and social circumstances can muffle or even obliterate texts, paintings, compositions, in which ill fortune or abnegation can keep worthwhile work buried. But generally considered, there is no muteness in the poet. Whatever its stature, the poem speaks; it speaks out; it speaks to. The meaning, the existential modes of art, music and literature are functional within the experience of our meeting with the other. All aesthetics, all critical and hermeneutic discourse, is an attempt to clarify the paradox and opaqueness of that meeting as well as its felicities. The ideal of complete echo, of translucent reception is, exactly, that of the messianic. For in the messianic dispensation, every semantic motion and marker would become perfectly intelligible truth; it would have the life-naming, life-giving authority of great art when it reaches the one for whom it is uniquely intended – and here, 'uniquely' does not mean 'solely'.

The unbounded diversities of formal articulation and stylistic construct correspond to the unbounded diversities of the modes of our meeting with the other. It is a commonplace of ethnography that early, 'primitive' art forms were meant to tempt towards domesticity, towards familiarity, the animal presences in the great dark of the outside world. Cave paintings are talismanic and propitiatory rites performed to make of the encounter with the teeming strangeness and menace of organic presences a source of mutual recognition and of benefit. The marvels of penetrative mimesis on the bison-walls at Lascaux are solicitations: they would draw the opaque and brute force of the 'thereness' of the non-human into the luminous ambush of representation and understanding. All representations, even the most abstract, infer a rendezvous with intelligibility or, at the least, with a strangeness attenuated, qualified by observance and willed form. Apprehension (the meeting with the other) signifies both fear and perception. The continuum between both, the modulation from one to the other, lie at the source of poetry and the arts.

But if much of poetry, music and the arts aims to 'enchant' – and we must never strip that word of its aura of magical summons – much also, and of the most compelling, aims to make strangeness in certain respects stranger. It would instruct us of the inviolate enigma of the otherness in things and in animate presences. Serious painting, music, literature or sculpture make palpable to us, as do no other means of communication, the unassuaged, unhoused instability and estrangement of our condition. We are, at key instants, strangers to ourselves, errant at the gates of our own psyche. We knock blindly at the doors of turbulence, of creativity, of inhibition within the *terra incognita* of our own selves. What is more unsettling: we can be, in ways almost unendurable to reason, strangers to those whom we would know best, by whom we would be best known and unmasked.

Beyond the strength of any other act of witness, literature and the arts tell of the obstinacies of the impenetrable, of the absolutely alien which we come up against in the labyrinth of intimacy. They tell of the Minotaur at the heart of love, of kinship, of uttermost confiding. It is the poet, the composer, the painter, it is the religious thinker and metaphysician when they give to their findings the persuasion of form, who instruct us that we are monads haunted by communion. They tell us of the irreducible weight of otherness, of enclosedness, in the texture and phenomenality of the material world. Only art can go some way towards making accessible, towards waking into some measure of communicability, the sheer inhuman otherness of matter – it haunted Kant – the retractions out of reach of rock and wood, of metal and of fibre (let the metal of a Brancusi figure sing to your hand). It is poetics, in the full sense, which inform us of the visitor's visa in place and in time which defines our status as transients in a house of being whose foundations, whose future history, whose rationale – if any – lie wholly outside our will and comprehension. It is the capacity of the arts, in a definition which must, I believe, be allowed to include the living forms of the speculative (what tenable vision of poetics will exclude Plato, Pascal, Nietzsche?), to make us, if not at home, at least alertly, answerably peregrine in the unhousedness of our human circumstance. Without the arts, form would remain unmet and strangeness without speech in the silence of the stone.

Hence the immemorial logic of the relations between music, poetry and art on the one hand and the affront of death on the other. In death the intractable constancy of the other, of that on which we have no purchase, is given its most evident concentration. It is the facticity of death, a facticity wholly resistant to reason, to metaphor, to revelatory representation, which makes us 'guest-workers', *frontaliers*, in the boarding-houses of life. Where it engages, uncompromisingly, the issues of our condition, poetics seeks to elucidate the incommunicado of our meetings with death (in their terminal structure, narrations are rehearsals for death). However inspired, no poem, no painting, no musical piece – though music comes closest – can make us at home with death, let alone "weep it from its purpose". But it is within the compass of the arts that the metaphor of resurrection is given the edge of felt conjecture. The central conceit of the artist that the work shall outlast his own death, the existential truth that great literature, painting, architecture, music have survived their creators, are not accidental or self-regarding. It is the lucid intensity of its meeting with death that generates in aesthetic forms that statement of vitality, of life-presence, which distinguishes serious thought and feeling from the trivial and the opportunistic.

At a dread cost of personal means, at a risk more unforgiving of failure than any other – the saint, the martyr know their elected destination – the artist, the poet, the thinker as shaper, seek out the encounter with otherness where such otherness is, in its blank essence, most inhuman. Why should death concede times of chosen meeting when we are, in fact, all on the same road towards it? Why should it grant the largesse of three roads meeting between Thebes and Delphi? Yet poetry and art compel it to do so. And they exercise, they give endurable form to that coercion still, as neither politics nor the sciences can.

A reflection on or (as German grammar allows) 'a thinking of' meetings, of encounters as instrumentalities of communication, comports a morality. An analysis of enunciation and of signification – the signal to the other – entails an ethics. It is this entailment which may provide the first step out of the house of mirrors which is that of modernist theory and practice.

The relations of ethics to poetics have, since Plato's critique of the mendacities in Homer, been a source of fertile vexation. It is the merit of the Enlightenment, of Kant principally, to have sought to remove the domain of the aesthetic from that of systematic cognition on the one hand and from that of practical morality on the other. The Kantian postulate of the 'disinterestedness' of artistic and literary invention would distance the truth, the beauty, the liberties taken by the imaginary from the surveillance of moralistic criteria. This enfranchisement justly underlines the autonomous quality of the poetic act. It reminds us that the authenticity, the truth of motive in literature, in music, in the arts are indivisible from the executive form of the work, and that the verity of a poem or a painting is that of the specific internality and integrity of its shaping. The Kantian proposal of an extra-territoriality for the life of the arts is made both poignant and peremptory in Keats's identification of truth with beauty and of beauty with truth. In so far as this equation and the Kantian concept of the special freedom of the poetic, of the disinterestedness of the fictive, help us to see more clearly the authority and singularity of the aesthetic experience, they are of eminent value. At the same time, however, any thesis that would, either theoretically or practically, put literature and the arts beyond good and evil is spurious.

The archaic torso in Rilke's famous poem says to us: "change your life". So do any poem, novel, play, painting, musical composition worth meeting. The voice of intelligible form, of the needs of direct address from which such form springs, asks: 'What do you feel, what do you think of the possibilities of life, of the alternative shapes of being which are implicit in your experience of me, in our encounter?' The indiscretion of serious art and literature and music is total. It queries the last privacies of our existence. This interrogation, like the winding of the sudden horn at the dark tower in Browning's emblematic text of the seeking out of being by art, is no abstract dialectic. It purposes change. Early Greek thought identified the Muses with the arts and wonder of persuasion. As the act of the poet is met – and it is the full tenor and rites of this meeting which I would explore – as it enters the precincts, spatial and temporal, mental and physical, of our being, it brings with it a radical calling towards change. The waking, the enrichment, the complication, the darkening, the unsettling of sensibility and understanding which follow on our experience of art are incipient with action. Form is the root of performance. In a wholly fundamental, pragmatic sense, the poem, the statue, the sonata are not so much read, viewed or heard as they are *lived*. The encounter with the aesthetic is, together with certain modes of religious and of metaphysical experience, the most 'ingressive', trans-formative summons available to human experiencing. Again, the shorthand image is that of an Annunciation, of "a terrible beauty" or gravity breaking into the small house of our cautionary being. If we have heard rightly the wing-beat and provocation of that visit, the house is no longer habitable in quite the same way as it was before. A mastering intrusion has shifted the light (that is very precisely, non-mystically, the shift made visible in Fra Angelico's *Annunciation*).

Such shifts are organically enfolded within categories of good and evil, of humane and inhumane conduct, of creative and destructive enactment. Any mature representation of imagined form, any mature endeavour to communicate such represen-tation to another human being, is a moral act – where 'moral' can, unquestionably, include the articulation of sadism, of nihilism, of the bringing of unreason and despair. 'Art for art' is a tactical slogan, a necessary rebellion against philistine didacticism and political control. But pressed to its logical conse-quences, it is pure narcissism. The 'purest' work of art, the most abstemious from conceivable empirical instruction or appliance,

143

is, by virtue of that very purity and abstention, a sharply political gesture, a value-statement of the most evident ethical import. We cannot touch on the experiencing of art in our personal and communal lives without touching, simultaneously, on moral issues of the most compelling and perplexing order. Are the resources of production, display and reception expended on the arts in a given political structure and economy justifiable (Tolstoy came to believe that they were not)? Do the identifications with fictions, the inner, tidal motions of pathos and *libido* which the novel, the film, the painting, the symphony unleash within us somehow immunize us against the humbler, less formed, but actual claims of suffering and of need in our surroundings? Does the cry in the tragic play muffle, even blot out, the cry in the street? (I confess to finding this an obsessive, almost maddening question.) Coleridge thought so: "Poetry excites us to artificial feelings – makes us callous to real ones." What, if any, are the artist's responsibilities towards those whom his poems 'sent out to be shot' (Yeats) or, one must add, to shoot (Auden's celebration of "the necessary murder")? Are there any defensible limitations to the material, to the fantasies which literature, drama, painting or film can publish (can we conceive of serious art persuading our imaginings towards the torture or sexual abuse of children, a question made inescapable by certain moments in Dostoevsky)?

It is just because the persuasions to action in the aesthetic – most immediately if enigmatically in music – are so forceful, it is just because the fascinations and uprootings which images exercise on our conscious and subconscious motivations and springs of conduct are so far-reaching, that the question of constraint, of censorship, is, from Plato's *Republic* to the present, a far more challenging one than liberal instinct would allow. Or to put it another way: does an artist bear any responsibility whatever for the misuse, abuse, barbarization of his inventions? Lukács held Wagner to be implicated, to the end of time, in the uses to which Nazism put his music. Not one note in Mozart, he argued, could be so used. To which, when I reported this dictum to Roger Sessions, that most philosophically acute of modern composers replied by playing the opening bars of the aria of the Queen of the Night in *The Magic Flute*.

No serious writer, composer, painter has ever doubted, even in moments of strategic aestheticism, that his work bears on good and evil, on the enhancement or diminution of the sum of humanity in man and the city. To imagine originally, to shape into significant expression, is to test in depth those potentialities of understanding and of conduct ("thrones, dominions, powers" as the rhetoric and architecture of the baroque have it) which are the life-substance of the ethical. A message is being sent; to a purpose. The style, the explicit figurations of that message may be perverse, they may intend the subjugation, even the ruin of the recipient. They may claim for themselves, as in Sade, as in the black paintings of Goya, as in the death-dance of Artaud, the sombre licence of the suicidal. But their pertinence to questions and consequences of an ethical order is the more palpable. Only trash, only *kitsch* and artefacts, texts, music which are produced *solely* for monetary or propagandistic ends do, indeed, transcend (transgress) morality. Theirs is the pornography of insignificance.

But the problem I want to clarify now is a more particular one, and often unobserved. It is not so much that of the morality or amorality of the work of meaning and of art. It is that of the ethics of its reception. What are the moral categories relevant to our meetings with the poem, with the painting or the musical construct? In what respect are certain moral motions of sensibility essential to the communicative act and to our apprehension of

145

it? In Lorenzo Lotto's *Annunciation*, one of the most unsettling, haunting versions we have of this inexhaustible theme, the Lady turns her back on the rushing radiance of the Messenger. That, too, is possible.

2

Oriental manuals of decorum, etiquette books of the European Renaissance and Enlightenment dwell on welcome. They detail the nuances of idiom and of gesture which define varying degrees and intensities of reception. They tell us how different social classes, genders, generations may meet appropriately. From such ceremonies of reciprocal perception, an axis of meaning extends into metaphysics and theology. It passes through models of translation in the fullest sense of that decisive but always problematic act. Translation comprises complex exercises of salutation, of reticence, of commerce between cultures, between tongues and modes of saying. A master translator can be defined as a perfect host. So far as it analyses the conditions of awareness and of intelligibility between the ego and the other, between the one and the many, so far as its means are those of question and response, of proposition and examination, philosophy systematizes intuitions, impulses of both encounter and valediction. There is much to be parted from at the interruption or close of the philosophic act of discourse and the study of such parting is crucial to Epicurean doctrine, to Hegel's *Phenomenology*, to Wittgenstein's *Tractatus*. A number of modern thinkers, Buber and Lévinas most notably, argue a theory of meaning based on literal envisaging, this is to say of the vision we have of the face, of the expressive 'thereness' of the other human person. The 'open impenetrability' of that visage, its alien yet confirmatory mirroring of our own, enact the intellectual and ethical challenge of the relations of man to man and of man to that which Lévinas terms 'infinity' (the potentialities of relationship are always inexhaustible).

Great poetry is animate with the rites of recognition. Odysseus proceeds from one recognition to the next in a voyage towards the self that is Ithaca. Dante recognizes the timbre of Brunetto Latini's voice out of the ghost-smoke. Titania is "ill-met by moonlight". In turn, religious thought and practice metaphorize, make narrative images of, the rendezvous of the human psyche with absolute otherness, with the strangeness of evil or the deeper strangeness of grace. Salutations are to be deciphered: in Jacob's wrestling match and contest of nominations through the night, in the presence after presentness which is met on the road to Emmaus.

These intuitions and ceremonials of encounter, in social usage, in linguistic exchange, in philosophic and religious dialogue, are incisively pertinent to our reception of literature, of music and of the arts. They bear closely on our recognitions, on our *entente* (our hearing) of what the poem, the painting, the sonata would with us. We are the 'other ones' whom the living significations of the aesthetic seek out. It is on our capacities for welcome or refusal, for response or imperception, that their own necessities of echo and of presence largely depend. To think about why there should be painting or poetry or music at all – an order of matter and of being in which there would be none is perfectly conceivable – is to think about the kinds of entrance which we allow them or which they exact into the narrows of our individual existence.

Against the equation between text and commentary, making of aesthetic creation nothing but a 'pre-text', I want to test the instrumental force of the concept of courtesy. The root-strength of that word has ebbed. *Cortesia*, as it unfolds out of Christian romance and the Western formulations of 'courtly' love, carries a precise, probing wealth of associations. It tells of the chivalric, of the secret sovereignties of heart-to-heart, of reticence under pressure of revelation. Very concretely, the phenomenology of courtesy would organize, that is to say quicken into articulate life, our meetings with the other, with the beloved, with the adversary, with the familiar and the stranger. It would, on a tree of meaning, connect the only partially perceived encounters between our conscious and unconscious selves to those meetings which take place in the lit spaces of social, political and moral conduct. Classically, where branch and leaf are highest, *cortesia* qualifies the last ambush or the final tryst which is the possible venue – the coming, the coming to a place – of God. Inwoven in this sequence are certain courtesies towards, in the face of, death, without which our music, poetry and art would be shallow. Deconstruction has nothing to say of death. For death, says De Man, is merely "a displaced name for a linguistic predicament".

But the concept which I am trying to pin down is both more modest and elusive. I want to bring to bear on the question of our experiencing and understanding of meaningful form a moral intuition. Yet this also is too vague and exalted a term. I require, I do not quite know how to express a plainly intelligible category in which morality, courtesy, perceptive trust can be seen to be nothing more than the concentrate of common sense.

The informing agency is that of *tact*, of the ways in which we allow ourselves to touch or not to touch, to be touched or not to be touched by the presence of the other (the parable of doubting Thomas in the garden crystallizes the manifold mysteries of tact). The issue is that of civility (a charged word whose former strength has largely left us) towards the inward savour of things. What means have we to integrate that savour into the fabric of our own identity? We need a terminology which plainly articulates the intuition that an experience of communicated forms of meaning demands, fundamentally, a courtesy or tact of heart, a tact of sensibility and of intellection which are conjoined at their several roots.

We lay a clean cloth on the table when we hear the guest at our threshold. In the paintings of Chardin, in the poems of Trakl, that movement at evening is made both domestic and sacramental. We light the lamp at the window. The implicit impulses in such acts are precisely those in which the yearning towards and fear of the other, the motions of feeling and of thought which would, at the same time, guard and open outward their particular, individual dwelling, come together. Such impulses are known in immediacy. They cannot be formalized or 'proved' (no significant act of spirit can be). But they are of the essence, which is to say, essential.

I am, in short, seeking to define a notion as plain as daylight, yet as elusive and vulnerable as any in the *finesses* of psychology. It is both a courtly rubric and one as banal as a handshake. It is of a generality which encompasses something like toilet training at one end – much in deconstructive semiotics does playful dirt on the objects of its notice – all the way to the ceremonial gravities of the sacramental at the other. 'Courtesy of mind', 'scruple of perception', 'mannerliness of understanding' are rough approximations. But they are too specialized. Syntax balks at 'common-sense heart'. What we must focus, with uncompromising clarity, on the text, on the work of art, on the music before us, is an ethic of common sense, a courtesy of the most robust and refined sort.

The consequences are imperative platitudes. That they need re-stating is the precise gauge of our present situation.

I take it to be a moral and pragmatic fact that the poem,

the painting, the sonata, are prior to the act of reception, of commentary, of valuation. I say 'moral and pragmatic' simply because we lack the necessary word with which to fuse the most ordinary common sense with courtesy of heart and being. Though I am voicing an utter self-evidence, the nature, the compass of the priority of created form over our reception of its intelligible presence needs to be spelt out exactly.

There is priority in time. The poem comes before the commentary. The construct precedes the deconstruction. Temporality is a metaphysically and existentially resistant category. It has been sharply relativized in the world-view of modern science. Time can be bent into contingency and accident. There have been instances, though few, though suspect in their artifice, in which a picture, a literary text, a musical composition, have been realized in calculated response to some theoretical, critical, programmatic expectation. (At the ludicrous level, certain popular fictions have been manufactured *after* the film or television serial which had purported to be derived from them.) But normally – and here the reach of 'the norm' in that pale adverb is far stronger than eroded and concessionary usage declares – the bringing into being of the work of art is prior to all other modes of its subsequent existence. It has precedence; it has right of way.

"Being and time", says the philosopher. The two are indissoluble. Priority in time entails an essentiality in respect of the work itself and of what comes after. Outside Creation Myths there is no *Ur-werk*, no primordial, autochtonous, self-born act of aesthetic invention or formulation. Here deconstruction is perfectly right. The most radical originality occurs within a context, even if it is only that of the already extant language and of the neuro-physiological means and limitations of both human contrivance and reception (there are frequencies or pitches in light and sound which are outside our biological range). But the context of the creative determines that of the response, of the commentary. That determination has the force of causality. The poem, the picture, the composition is the *raison d'être*, the literal 'ground and rationale of being' of the interpretations and judgements which it elicits. It is, indeed, the 'pre-text' of all subsequent, related 'textualities', 'inter-textualities' (citations, allusions, *reprises*) and 'counter-textualities', but not in any trivializing, diminishing sense. It is their source of being. The temporal-ontological movement from the primary to the secondary is one from autonomy – within the constraints of human potentiality – to dependence. This is crucial.

We have seen that the commentary, the translation, the formal transformation or even the polemic parody of the source-text can surpass the original. Their brilliance can come to replace or to bury it. We have seen that modernist relativism is right when it insists on the fluidity of the lines which separate the vitality of the primary from that of the secondary. Yet neither truth alters the profound difference between the status of being of the independent and the dependent forms. The primary text – the poem, picture, piece of music – is a phenomenon *of freedom*. It can be or it cannot be. The hermeneutic-critical response, the executive enactment via performance, via vision and reading, are the clauses dependent on that freedom. Even at the highest point of recreative or subversive virtuosity, their genesis is that of dependence. Their licence may indeed be boundless (the post-structuralist and deconstructive game-theories and play have shown this); but their freedom is strictly a *secondary* one.

The grammatologist, the critic, the musical analyst, the art historian or iconographer practise their several liberties in answer to the work. They are 'about' the object of their consideration. If a serious work is truly generative of all its future readings and misreadings, the latter, however inventive in their own right, are not, or to discriminate with exceeding care, are not necessarily, are not by their own nature and essence, generative of any creation after them. Commentary breeds commentary: not new poems. There is not, in the truth-hour of his consciousness, a commentator, critic, aesthetic theorist, executant, however masterly, who would not have preferred to be a source of primary utterance and shaping. There have in Byzantine courts been all-powerful eunuchs, as there have been critics or deconstructionists magisterial over creation. But the basic distinction remains.

I have put forward this postulate on grounds of that courtesy of perception which is common sense, which is the tact of intuition, as it were, crystallized. I have made appeal to the self-awareness of ontological and logical dependence or 'secondarity' in even the most anarchic craftsman of echo. But this is only a preliminary step. Remaining entirely within the compass of secular, commonsensical, immanent orders of experience, of veracity, of self-consciousness, I now want to look more closely at the notion of 'freedom'. In our encounter with art and the meanings of art, in our responses to the offers and solicitations of intelligibility in fictive, autonomous forms, two categories of freedom seem to me decisively instrumental. Again, the one looks to be primary; the other sequent.

The experiencing of created form is a meeting between freedoms. The famous question at the roots of metaphysics is: "why should there not be nothing?". This very same question underlies any grasp of poetics and of art. The poem, the sonata, the painting, could very well *not* be. Except in the trivial, contingent perspective of the commission, of material need, of psychic coercion, the aesthetic phenomenon, the shaping act, is at all times and in all places at liberty not to come into being. This absolute gratuitousness entails precisely the disinterestedness of true art as Kant defined it. Nothing necessitates the generation of the fictive (Plato wrestles with this anarchic spontaneity, and Aristotle seeks to anchor it to our mimetic animality). In the immense majority of adult men and women, early impulses towards the making of art have withered away altogether. The production of executive forms by the sculptor, composer or poet is a supremely free act. It is liberality in essence and, rigorously considered, a wholly unpredictable choice not not to be.

As rudimentary sagacity has it, we know neither of our coming nor of our going hence. We are inmates, not begetters or masters, of our lives. Yet the indistinct intimation of a lost freedom or of a freedom to be regained – Arcadia behind us, Utopia before – hammers at the far threshold of the human psyche. This shadowy pulsebeat lies at the heart of our mythologies and of our politics. We are creatures at once vexed and consoled by summons of a freedom just out of reach. In one domain the experience of freedom is deployed. In one sphere of the human circumstance, to be is to be at liberty. It is that of our encounter with music, art and literature.

This is the case at the most negative level. We are utterly free not to receive, not to meet with authentic aesthetic modes at all. Even as it forgets or represses the formative drives of childhood, so the immense majority of mankind will experience the solicitations of literature and of the arts only very rarely. Or they will answer to such solicitations only in their most ephemeral, narcotic guise (narcotic in precisely the sense in which trash is, itself, calculated, profitable, interested and, therefore, unfree). Nothing lies nearer to daily hand than the bypassing, the blank imperception of the poem or painting. Taste of *any* kind, together with the numbing of taste and the abstention of notice from the demands of quality, is a universal human right – where 'right' is the essential antithesis to 'freedom'. Given a free vote, this is to say the option to spend its leisure and economic resources as it wishes, the overwhelming plurality of mankind, as I have already said, will elect bingo or the television chat-show over Aeschylus or Giorgione. This is the absolute right of the un-free. And it is one of the laming necessities of liberal and democratic theories, bound as they are to the freedom of the market, that they must safeguard and institutionalize this right.

The crux lies at another level. Where seriousness meets with seriousness, exigence with exigence, in the ontological and ethical spaces of the disinterested, where art and poetics, impera-tively contingent in their own coming into being and intelligible form, meet the receptive potential of a free spirit, there takes place the nearest we can know of the existential realization of freedom. It takes, as it were, two freedoms to make one. Two analogies may help to elucidate the point. Theology and speculative metaphysics engage the possibilities of meeting or of non-meeting with the 'other' in its transcendent guise. The second analogy is that of the erotic, of our meeting or refusal of meeting with the other in the incidence of love (or of hatred). Analogously, the reception or denial of the aesthetic presence engages an exchange of liberties, of liberties given and taken. There is a profound suggestion in the idiom whereby some eminent man or woman is given the 'freedom of the city', in which he is invited to enter its gates in order to be pre-eminently at home, at liberty therein.

A further clarification is needed. Inquiry in the pure and the natural sciences does exemplify a comparable free space. But not altogether. The objects of scientific speculation and investi-gation, however uncertain their reality-status outside the relevant hypothesis and observation, are, nevertheless, *given*. They are prior and determinant in ways which differ fundamentally from the 'coming-into-thereness' of the aesthetic. The choices made in the sciences, the forward motion of the collective scientific enterprise, are phenomenologically imposed as those in the sonata or novel are not. Thus it may be that only pure mathematics, whose kinship with music so exercised Pythagorean and Platonic meditation, is phenomenally free, 'at liberty', in the manner of the arts. Yet even here, application threatens. Only in the aesthetic is there the absolute freedom 'not to have come into being'. Paradoxically, it is that possibility of absence which gives autonomous force to the presence of the work.

Where freedoms meet, where the integral liberty of donation or withholding of the work of art encounters our own liberty of reception or refusal, *cortesia*, what I have called tact of heart, is of the essence. The numinous intimations which relate hospitality to religious feeling in countless cultures and societies, the intuition that the true reception of a guest, of a known stranger in our place of being touches on transcendent obligations and opportunities, helps us to understand the experiencing of created form. It is these obligations and opportunities which I want to circumscribe precisely in the definition of *philology*. Again, I will do so, at first, on a purely secular, even technical level. I will be illustrating the philological enactment of our experience of meaningful forms with reference to verbal constructs, to texts. But this reference always extends to our readings of the sculpture, of the painting, of the architectural composition, of the musical shape. The disciplines of courtesy are the same. They can, in shorthand, be mapped as instrumental in the spaces of sensibility between two insights: Valéry's dictum that syntax is a constituent element of the human spirit, and the observation of the seventeenth-century theologian and metaphysician, Malebranche, that rigorous attention is "the natural piety of the soul".

Face to face with the presence of offered meaning which we call a text (or a painting or a symphony), we seek to hear its language. As we would that of the elect stranger coming towards us. There is in this endeavour, as deconstruction would immediately point out, an ultimately unprovable hope and presupposition of sense, a presumption that intelligibility is conceivable and, indeed, realizable. Such a presupposition is always susceptible of refutation. The presence before us may be that of a mute (Beckett edges us towards that grim jest), of a madman uttering gibberish or, more disturbingly, of an intensely communicative persona whose idiom – linguistic, stylistic, hermetically-grounded – we simply cannot grasp. There are literary, artistic, musical works which remain closed or only superficially accessible to even the most welcoming of perceptions. In short, the movement towards reception and apprehension does embody an initial, fundamental act of trust. It entails the risk of disappointment or worse. As we shall note, the guest may turn despotic or venomous. But without the gamble on welcome, no door can be opened when freedom knocks.

Where the poem, where the verbal construct is concerned, the opening of the door, the practices of courtesy which this motion of trust comports, are those of lexical-grammatical-formal study. We strive to achieve the greatest possible degree of accurate audition. If the poem is speaking out of our own tongue, we seek to ascertain the historical, social, if need be local or dialectal, status of the poet's particular idiom. If the text is in a foreign language – and there is no more concentrated instance of 'otherness' and of its freedom of being than that of our encounters with languages not our own – we do our laboured best either to master that other speech or to accept the humbling trust of translation. Each step in this proceeding of 'entrances and alarms' has its own exactions and harvest.

Lexical *cortesia*, the first step in philology, is that which makes us dwellers in the great dictionaries, both general and specialized. It is that which opens to us the theological, political and regional vocabulary of Dante, his *Wortschatz* (literally 'word-hoard', which is the mode of the gift he brings us). The lexical makes palpable to us the legal, military, botanical and crafts-man's vocabularies and reference-nets with which Shakespeare draws in the prodigal precisions of his word-world. We learn to hear the alchemy in Goethe, the argot in Joyce. The exercise and yield are of the order of articulation of meaning as it obtains in music. A natural, persistent recourse to the *Oxford English Dictionary*, to the French Littré, enables us to *hear* the unfolding of historical continuity and of change inside words themselves and within the bodies of text in which these words are organic.

It takes a distinct musicality of interpretative hearing, an ear for temporal tuning such as we find in Coleridge, in Walter Benjamin, in William Empson, to hear, to register with near-perfect or perfect pitch the life of time and of structure within words. It takes close listening to the poem, to the dramatic dialogue or descriptive passage in the novel to glean from the single word or phrase the harvest of preceding history, of transmutations within connotations and even root-meanings. Gradually the finesse of our reception increases. We come to identify the germ of novelty, of personal appropriation and of re-routing which a word or a phrase may be given by the usage of the particular writer, by the purposive dynamics of the particular text.

The profit of insight (the intensity of encounter) is major. Via lexical tact, the reader-listener comes to discriminate, almost subliminally, between, say, the weight, rugosities, range, 'feel' of the same word – but it is not the same – in a passage of Milton, in one of Marvell, in one of Dryden, written, and there lies the fascination, at very nearly the identical date. It is lexica which tell us at what moments after Kant the word 'judgement', be it in Wordsworth or Vigny, takes on a new tonality, or at what crossroads after Freud 'consciousness' alters pace, density and echo. Literature is, as Mallarmé insisted, made of words. In the sober rites of reception which I call 'philological', the lexical is, literally (itself an enigmatically-charged adverb), the first confiding.

The second stage of philological reception demands an exact sensitivity to syntax, to the grammars which are the sinew of articulate forms. It is via grammar, in the deepest sense, that meaning enters, that it steps into the light of accountable presence. Today, linguists argue about the psychological-formal depths at which the springs, the first lineaments of syntax lie. Some would locate them at a level comparable, in more than image, to the sequences, rules and punctuations of the genetic code. But even if there are universal constraints on the generation of grammatical sentences, and this remains to be proved, the branchings which innervate and construe the means of natural language (they change historically) are beyond enumeration or formalization. The ways in which different tongues map and segment the phenomenal, the ways in which they situate experiences in time and space – the tenses, the moods of the verb – are direct grammatical options and performative acts. They differ fundamentally as between cultures and epochs. Anthropology parses the radically diverse systems of nomination and gender, of pronominal substitution which underlie, which, in fact, make conceivable, kinship structures and social relations. Hebraic intemporality in regard to prophecy and to God's eternal 'thereness' – yesterday and tomorrow are now, are 'presently' – is organically situated in the a-temporal and horizontal mode of Hebrew verbs. It is almost a truism to say that the harsh clarity, the rage for definition and the terminal (*perfectum*) in Roman law and the legal systems which derive from it, are the codification in familial and public life of the rules of Latin syntax. The "perpendicularity to the fact" which Stendhal so prized in the *Code Napoléon* and which, in turn, is the armature of his own prose, is a matter of grammar. The grammarian-reader, in the sense I am trying to delineate, hears, feels the means of meaning beneath the skin. He encounters the nerve and bone structure beneath the verse and the sentence, beneath the spatial and chromatic relations on the canvas, beneath the dimensions of the nave. He learns to hear the key-relations and pitch that are the grammar of music.

We have, to a large extent, lost this feel. The realization of the medieval speculative grammarians that the human pulse of time and of identity was rooted in grammar, that the world of man and of woman is, in a sense nearly Wittgensteinian, a grammatical construct consonant either with material verity or with the relational properties of our minds or with both, is distant from us. Many of us, conventionally literate, can no longer parse an ordinary sentence, let alone analyse the functions of parts of speech which were once standard school lore. Innocent of syntactic sensibility and training, we hardly register the dynamic tensions between that in language which is conservative, which seeks legitimacy in precedent and the useful fiction of 'correctness', and that which is innovative and creatively illicit. A genuine grammaticality of understanding is the very opposite to any thick-skinned and naïve espousal of lasting rules (there are none across time). It is, on the contrary, a fascinated, informed perception of that which changes in the anatomy of style and of speech, which changes in the grammars of tonality or atonality in music. Grammars are rebelliously alive. A dead or contracting language, a dead or contracting aesthetic manner, are precisely those in which the syntactical legislation has become monumentally atrophied, in which trespass can no longer quicken enshrined life. (A deep-lying bias towards such monumentality gives to French, in contrast to Anglo-American, much of its vulnerable *dignitas* and defensiveness.)

There is a part of rhetoric in every communicative act and visitation. Rhetoric is the craft of charging with significant effect the lexical and grammatical units of utterance. A statue, a building, have their rhetoric of self-presentment. So does the sound-structure and projection in a piece of music. The actual proceedings of persuasion are built of the relevant grammar. Metaphor, metonymy, synecdoche, the tropes of pathos or of irony without which our speech would stale into that of tautology and of the computer, are actions of syntax. An anaphoric arrangement, that is to say the sequent reiteration of certain phrases towards a cumulative or a diminishing effect (consider Biblical doublets), is grammar in movement. As are the repetitions of a motif in music, of an ornament or structural feature in a building. Lacking an unforced feel for the vitalities of grammar, we have all but lost any valuation of the rhetorical. Indeed, a vaguely pejorative sheen now attaches to the term. This means that major spheres of Western literature, from Pindar to Cicero, from Cicero to the Victorians, spheres which are, in the best sense, ceremonial, explicitly eloquent, formal in their idiom of address, are accessible to us only in the grey of scholarship or historical conservation. Challengingly (I do not know any explanation), parallel energies of rhetoric, of oratory, in baroque art and music, in modern painting – has there been a more deliberate, cunning rhetorician than Picasso? – have met with a far wider reception than any granted to discourse.

But it is just in our experience of poetry, of language in its most expressive guise, that is to say in literature, that a natural welcome to grammar is most fruitful and an incapacity for such welcome most damaging. Roman Jakobson's dictum prevails: the poetry of grammar is the grammar of poetry. There is, quite simply, not a serious literary text in any tongue, genre or tradition which would not make the point.

If one is to give true welcome, into one's own small granary of feeling and of understanding, to the exchanges between Oberon and Titania, between Oberon and Puck in *A Midsummer Night's Dream* (II,i) – and language hardly knows a more joyful knock at one's door – one must be able to hear grammar made music. The issue is the rare participial boldness of Titania's "childing"; it is that of one's grasp of the wondrous aptness of Oberon's "throned *by* the west", where commonplace 'throned *in*' would not do. The attempt must be made to elucidate grammatically "There sleeps Titania sometime of the night" so as to tease out of *sometime of* an intelligible part – even the subtlest grammarian-listener can do no more – of its technical magic, of that which makes the footfall of meaning enigmatically lustrous as would no other syntactic turn or 'deviance' from the eroded and expected in daily usage.

Wallace Stevens's "Anecdote of the Jar" is a focal moment in modern literature and thought (that focus being its theme). Laconically, the three quatrains address our eyes, ears, tactile reflexes, as much as they do our cerebrations – a justly ugly word. The last three lines proclaim that

> The jar was gray and bare.
> It did not give of bird or bush,
> Like nothing else in Tennessee.

That "give", together with "nothing else", is at the edge of 'normal' syntax. It seems to impede our reception and acceptance of what is being said. It deconstructs, in turn, even the most provisional of paraphrases. Had Stevens written 'anything else', the crux of singularity, of urgent exploration, formal as well as substantive, would have been trivialized or altogether missed. We apprehend, by teased approximation, certain main currents of meaning: the bare 'nullity', its greyness ("Like nothing else"), centres, by mere *fiat* of chosen shape, the wilderness of unformed reality. But Stevens's 'counter-grammar' keeps us off balance. We know and do not know. We bend closer to the speaker as to a guest or traveller whose voice tires. A rich undecidability draws us. This is, to be sure, the poet's design. Grammatical normality 'fails' where meaning is set free.

The third level of the experiencing of form, as philology seeks adequate response, is that of the semantic. The term points to the aggregate and comprehensive product of signification of all lexical, grammatical and formal means. It denotes the executive passage of means into meaning. But this passage is incommensurable, simply because the units of communication in any given instance – the words, the syntax, the formal arrangement, the relevant material or notational code – enter immediately into a context. Once they are enunciated, they draw upon, they interact with the substantive and formal totality of the preceding and surrounding world. The context of a line in Shakespeare, of a sentence in *Madame Bovary* is, in the most demonstrable sense, unbounded. It is that of the whole of the English or French language, both diachronically, this is to say in its previous history, and synchronically, which means in reference to all conceivable contemporary values, connotations and usages. Its context is that of the ambient society and of the structure of that society in regard to other historical and social traditions. Context entails the history and life-forms of analogous and contrasting aesthetic genres. The potentialities of pertinent signification around a verse in a Shakespearian play are those of the manifold interpenetrations of the lyric and the dramatic. A Flaubert sentence implicates, as it were, the precedent of prose fiction as a whole and of the lyric and dramatic modes from which prose fiction abstains or, in Flaubert's case, which it internalizes within its own claims to surpassing universality. The circles of informing context spread concentrically to the unbounded. There is a sense, perfectly concrete, in which an exhaustive, a tautological analysis and understanding of any semantic or semiotic act would be an analysis and understanding of the sum total of being itself. However deep the trust and the disclosure, there are things about our visitant that we shall never know.

But the fact that there cannot be, in Coleridge's macaronic phrase, any *omnium gatherum* of the context that is the world, does not mean that intelligibility is either wholly arbitrary or self-erasing. Such deduction is nihilistic sophistry.

Context is at all times dialectical. Our reading modifies, is in turn modified by, the communicative presence of its object. This vitalizing reciprocity extends far beyond any formal, technical order. It is not only the case that the new poem alters the significations and conditions of reception of previous poetry or that a Braque 'abstract' still-life re-organizes, i.e. makes organic in a new structural and rhetorical relation of modes, the still-life by Chardin and by Cézanne. It is that all semantic-aesthetic phenomena, all acts of meaning out of verbal, material or acoustic form, are themselves of the informing context of our lives in the manifold of being. They are experience-data of historical, social, psychic existentiality as intense, as transformative, indeed often more so, than any other categories of encountered phenomenality. It is not only, as Wilde proclaimed, that nature imitates art. Nature comports art, both inwardly, in the inner spaces of our imaginings, desires, mappings of reality, and in the constructs of reality which surround us. Architecture is, self-evidently, landscape. But so, in degrees of increasing psychological internalization, are paintings, statues, verbal representations of the human and the natural manner of things and, most subtly, those musical dispositions of time and of space which, in ways we fully experience even if we cannot as yet rationalize them, change the felt pulse of our daily lives. The streets of our cities *are* different after Balzac and Dickens. Summer nights, notably to the south, have changed with Van Gogh. Fascinatingly, aleatory and electronic music are giving a new formal character and audibility to many of the urban, technological 'noises' which surround us. Thus, and centrally, the history of context in respect of meaning is the context of human history. The interactive proceedings between them are in perpetual, finally incommensurable motion.

It follows that we cannot devise a systematic theory of meaning in any but a metaphoric sense. Meaning is, in terms of proof, no more decidable, no more subject to the arrest of experimental demonstration than is the purpose (if there is any such) or 'sense' of our lives in the unbounded script of time and the world. In no theoretical or experimental mode can we make accountable to analytic proof our coming into being or death. This unaccountability is the essence of freedom. It is the compelling licence of imagining and of thought. Literature, art, music are the willed compactions of that freedom. Their open-endedness to understanding or misprision, to welcome or rejection, their inexhaustibility, are the best access we have to the 'otherness', to the freedom, at once bracing and abyssal, of life itself. When we give poetry, music, art entry into our being (the 'freedom of our city') we look on the naked presence – it can have an inhuman mien – of freedom itself. Therefore radical doubts, such as those of deconstruction and of the aesthetic of misreadings, are justified when they deny the possibility of a systematic, exhaustive hermeneutic, when they deny any arrival of interpretation at a stable, demonstrable singleness of meaning. But between this illusory absolute, this finality which would, in fact, negate the vital essence of freedom, and the gratuitous play, itself despotic by its very arbitrariness, of interpretative non-sense, lies the rich, legitimate ground of the philological.

3

The rites, the mythologies of welcome in human cultures comport an initial question. It is Farinata's high query of Dante: *"Chi fuor li maggior tui?"* We ask the guest to declare his provenance and the nature of his journey across time. This is no idle inquisition. The answer will tell us of the difficulty and liberality of his coming. The temporal, historical context of meaning, of articulate and executive forms, is integral to our possibilities of reception and response. No doubt, the right intimation and use of that context is always problematical and, in some sense, circular. If history is the informing circumference of a literary, artistic or musical act, this act, in turn, shapes and animates what we postulate as recapturable, documented historicity. In elusive essence, our experienced reconstructions of the past are grammatical and textual 'truth-fictions'. They are carpentered out of the availabilities of the past tense. No finally external verification attaches to them. Even the most neutral of archaeological or archival vestiges is made so by risk of interpretation, of the exercise of selective re-imagining which it engenders. Nor – and this is where Marxist methods need the most stringent safeguard – will even the most densely circumstantial historical context 'explain' the coming into dated being, let alone the intent and significations at the time, of a poem or painting or symphony. No documentation, where each document is a speech-act susceptible of interpretative reconstruction and deconstruction, in respect of what we now take to be the *accelerando* of time-feelings during and after the French Revolution, will provide us with any reliable causality in regard to the dramatization of pace and dimension in the sonatas or symphonies of Beethoven. Frequently, chronology deceives: Tennyson and Rimbaud are contemporaries.

But these are fertile traps. We are, ourselves, immersed in partly inherited, partly innovative and ideological categories of history. We bring to our readings, to our visions, to our hearings of aesthetic (formal) intelligibility both expectations and incomprehensions. The horizons of our understanding, the ways in which we situate in reference to ourselves the pastness of a text or work of art, our willed or enforced abolitions of this pastness under pressure of a revealed, sometimes insistent immediacy (the guest has his foot in our door), constitute the dynamic unsayabilities of the very experience of meaning. It is just the paradox whereby certain texts or musical compositions or paintings of our own day or of the most fully recollected yesterday have nothing to say to us, whereas others, immemorially remote, address us in the intimate vivacity of the instant, which confirms the freedom, the exchange between freedoms, which is the foundation of the aesthetic.

Knowing this, cognizant at every stage of the partly fictive nature of all historical evidence (of its own deconstructible textuality), we will, none the less, avail ourselves of what illumination there is.

The notion, developed during the 1940s by the New Criticism, of the total synchronicity of poetic texts, the refusal to date or historicize them lest any such location distort the purity of our aesthetic reflex, is a useful pedagogic trick. But it is nothing more. Language, style, instrumentation, the materiality of an architectural design or of a fresco, are grounded in historical temporality. The possibilities of realization, the necessities implicit in that grounding – the late medieval city-state with reference to Dante's *Commedia*, the inception of mercantilism and secular modernity as ambient to Shakespeare, the congruence between photographic collage, between the cinematographic liberties of placement and Surrealism – are of the utmost pertinence. The actual perception of what is textual, of what is mimetic presentment or abstraction, alerts across history. Chamber music can only develop with the concomitant availability of certain private or semi-private spaces for performance and audition. This availability is itself a matter of social-economic history, of the politics and of the finance of leisure. A good reading, a reading within freedom, will always be 'timeless'. This is to say that our endeavour at welcome, our questioning, will always take place *now*, in the presentness of a presence. But this immediacy is historically informed. Where our encounter is with that which speaks out of the past, we know that the idiom, the formal conventions, the aura of connotation and reference, are no longer ours. They must, in greater or lesser degree, be learnt, be 'looked up'. Though both may come to lodge compellingly in the inmost of our current, personal existence, the Pindaric ode and the realistic novel cannot be heard in the same performative register. Electronic reproduction and emission have made our sense of baroque music very distinctly ours. But we seek to refine this appropriation to the best of our (limited, suspect) abilities by learning something of the circumstances, social, political, technical, under which a Vivaldi or a Couperin composed. It would be inane arbitrariness and a gratuitous violence offered to common sense, to the moral-technical tact of reception, to dissociate Russian nineteenth-century literature, from Pushkin to Tolstoy, from the crowding context of social-political crises. Even at its most rigorous, Russian semantic and grammatological formalism never practised such dissociation. An overtly historical, even propagandistic painting, such as Delacroix's allegory on revolutionary tumult, is no more 'historical', is no more intensely a product of and against its temporal circumstance, than is an abstract, a 'white on white', by Malevich. Both tell of the time-bound and intemporal substance of meaning when meaning is formalized into communicable shape. Reciprocally, the planes and volumes in Delacroix's *Triumph of Liberty* are as susceptible of formal-theoretical examination as are those in the 'emptiness' of Malevich.

The argument extends to the closely-related sphere of the sociological. Well before Marx and such nineteenth-century positivists as Taine and Sainte-Beuve, Dr Johnson had underlined the social matrix in literature and the arts. Language as a medium, the interplay between social constraints and personal invention, the relations between artist, patron and public, are radically social. They embody class and commerce. It is abstruse nonsense to try and experience Blake without knowledge, however imperfect, of the complicated solitudes within social class which fuel the inspired idiosyncrasies of his artisanship and vision. The sociology of marginality in regard to religion and personal background is as crucial to a reading of Donne as it is to one of Proust. A thorough study of the effects of private income on certain forms and periods of aesthetic creation would enlighten us about vital elements in, say, Turgenev, Henry James, Paul Cézanne or Thomas Mann. Society is as contextual to the lives of sense and of form as these are to the development of society. The chemistry of reciprocal interpenetration is too manifold, too incommensurable to be systematically, let alone predictively (the Marxist claim), analysed and reconstituted. But it is insistently at work and we dim our chances of understanding, of welcome, if we overlook it.

The resort of philology to the biographical, to the intentionalities of the writer or artist or composer, is a minefield. Intuition cries out, reason makes more than plausible that there must be, that there are, functional relations between the maker and his making. How could it be otherwise? How could the form and purpose of the work not arise out of the life of the craftsman? But it is the nature of any such relationship, it is the presumption of causality which resists any ready demonstration and induces circularity of argument. Aristophanes may, at heart, have been the saddest of men – the which proposal is itself a piece of romanticized inversion. Our persuasion that some deep turbulence of spirit and sexuality attended on the composition of *King Lear* and *Timon of Athens* may be nothing but trivial rationalization. We have no shred of evidence either way.

Notions of causality are especially suspect in regard to the creative conventionalities and, as it were, anonymities in literature, music and the arts which precede the modern, this is to say the late-eighteenth-century and Romantic cultivation of the ego. In these classical modes professionalism pre-empts personality. Even where we can infer or document the facts, their full implications escape our modern view. It is likely that Shakespeare added the Fool, as we know him, to the script of *King Lear* at a late stage and for purely contingent, professional motives (the addition to his company of a "sweet-voiced" boy-actor and dancer). At the very last moment, Mozart made modifications of and addenda to *Don Giovanni* which seem to us of the essence, but whose actual reasons we know to have been technical or 'box-office'. The spectrum of conceivable interactions between the life and the work, the philosophically and semantically uncertain status of the self as figure of thought and of speech, are too fluid, too linguistically labile, to allow of any deterministic connection.

There is, moreover, a genuine sense in which aesthetic acts are accidents, are 'happenings', whose primary namelessness is disguised by the hazard of an individual signature. The language of the poem precedes and 'speaks' the poet more than it is formed or spoken by him. Numerous are the builders, painters, sculptors of the Middle Ages and early Renaissance known to us only as 'the Master' of this or that work. Music often seems to 'pass through' (though that is, again, a rhetorical figure) the person of its composer as it does through that of the performer with a formal necessity and universality far exceeding any individuation. It is only since pre-Romanticism that textuality and art are almost kindred to self-projection and the singular voice. Such self-projection is, more often than not, the move of the minor craftsman, of the tactics of the hour whose inherent weakness is, precisely, that of originality.

I have referred to the epistemological trap. The model of stable consciousness, of intentionality in regard to form and meaning, is, as we have seen, under acute critical pressure. We have seen what it means or, more strictly, what is the claim of 'non-meaning' when we invoke individual authorship and the intent of the definable psyche after Rimbaud, Nietzsche and Freud. It may be that Western aesthetics began with the anonymous, collective tenor of the oral epic and the dance, and that they are ending with the no less anonymous and collective phenomenology of the self-destruct piece of art, of aleatory music, of automatic writing (where 'automatic' includes not only the experiments of the Surrealists but the programmed commercialization of literature in a mass market). "Perfection of the life or of the work," said Yeats. It is immediately after this classical and stoic dissociation that both terms are held to be dramatic fictions, tropes calling for deconstruction.

Once more, the issue is one of the *cortesia* which perception owes, though always with self-questioning scruple, to common sense. The refusal to register, to take into account as a contributory energy of context, what we can gather of the artist's life, is a pretentious artifice. Such knowledge may be no more than ancillary. It need not, it must not obtrude on the immediacies of our trials of relation and response to the work itself. But drawn upon sceptically, provisionally, such knowledge will complicate and enrich these trials precisely as will a deepening familiarity with the life of the human beings we meet in dialogue. The good fortune of near-anonymity which characterizes a 'Homer' or, to a surprising degree, a Shakespeare, simply does not apply to many other creators. We may well be misconstruing the continuities or breaks in continuity between, for instance, the bodily infirmities and religious situation of Pope on the one hand and the voice of his elegies and satires on the other; but our misconstructions (our misreadings of the pendulum motion) are worth attempting and will bring to our answerability a more patient wealth. No musicology, no neuro-physiology as yet available, can relate for us, in any causal sense, the facts of Beethoven's deafness to the texture, tonality and intent of his later music. But our awareness of the paradox of deafness, our persistent though frustrated endeavours to give it meaningful play within our response to the compositions, are an existential truth. To read Proust well on the assumption of a mechanical, if adroitly masked, reversal of markers as between his own homoeroticism and the feminine identity of the beloved in the fiction, as between the actual Alfred and the imagined Albertine, is impossible. To read Proust well without knowing something of his personal condition and of the bearings of that condition on his conceptions of language, of society, of the art of the novel, is well-nigh impossible in a less crass but equally diminishing way.

Philology will, with self-ironizing alertness to the verbal, conventionally stylized nature of such relations, seek to enlist the matter of life in its readings of the matter of art. It will acknowledge the provocation, itself labyrinthine, itself an ironic solicitation to misconstruction, of Flaubert's: *"Emma Bovary, c'est moi."* It will do so knowing full well (as responsible sensibility has done long before the modern crisis of meaning) that in any such equation the dynamics of transformational interchange between the self and the otherness of the fictive persona can never be arrested, can never be resolved by any biographical inference. But knowing also that the suppression of such inference is a reductive discourtesy.

A resort to intentionality, to what we can say of the writer's or artist's purpose, sets traps even worse than those which attach to the uses of biography. Balaam – and Marx will cite this parable in his own exploration of the ideological contradictions inside literature – prophesies against his express will. An artist may deceive himself radically as to his true motives (where such 'truth' may, itself, be an epistemological phantom) and intended effects. He may, in Aesopian strategies, seek to deceive others (the censors). His most private diaries, letters, programme notes, may be rhetorical fictions within the genesis of fiction. Kafka's journals and conversations are masterworks of pained indirection in respect not only of others, but principally of himself. Their apparent translucence makes the actual work more secret. When Gide publishes his journal of the composition of *The Counterfeiters*, when Thomas Mann adds to *Doktor Faustus* the 'private' chronicle of its inception and elaboration, they are joining 'meta-texts' to texts. The articulate candour of these secondary statements carries no privileged truth-values. Thus we are bidden to "trust the tale and not the teller". But we require no deconstructive warning to signal to us the many-layered intentionalities of the tale itself, to remind us of the rhetorical incommensurabilities and self-dissolutions inherent in semantic acts. Schleiermacher's famous postulate whereby the reader can make out more of the authentic intent and significance of the text than could its author is fundamental to modern hermeneutics. It sets a wary transgression at the heart of interpretation.

Deconstruction has, in logical turn, undermined Schleier-macher's confident paradox. It has shown its circularity. Neither the expression of an author's or artist's putative intentions nor the re-interpretation, the possible refutation of these by his readers or viewers, have any stable, evidential status. The wounds of possibility, to use Kierkegaard's image, always remain open. Psychoanalysis seeks bedrock. It would tease out the motivations, the buried motions of necessity and meaning in the raw material of the psyche. It is these, claims the psycho-analytic reading, which the artist's professed intentionalities have concealed both from himself and his drowsy public. Via systematic distrust, psychoanalysis aims at a final confiding. I have already expressed my doubts, my belief that the revelations brought to daylight by the psychoanalytic mining of aesthetic and poetic forms are themselves fictions and mythical scenarios. Going further, one might observe that the dogma of verticality in all psychoanalytic readings, the wager on the authenticity of depths, are unresponsive to, irresponsible towards numerous categories of literature and the arts. There are countless texts, paintings, statues – perhaps even the *Moses* of Michelangelo so talismanic to Freud – whose strength, whose enunciations of organized sense, lie 'at the surface'. This might, indeed, be a first definition of the 'classical'. Nor has psychoanalysis had anything but faltering banalities to say about the relations between intent and encoding, between surface and depth, in music. But there, as I am arguing throughout, lies the crux of any account of the human experience of form as meaning.

None the less, both deconstructive negation and the promises of the psychoanalytic are to be heeded. They remind us of the circularities, of the processes of infinite regression implicit in any invocation of a writer's or artist's motives and stated intentions. The structures of language, the formalizations of art and of music, are those of indeterminacy. Intentionalities, even of the most confessional or programmatic sort, are rhetorical, grammatological moves. They 'take in' the self and the world, and we cannot escape the connotations of willed or subconscious duplicity inherent in that idiom. At some final level, the freedom we encounter when we read the poem, see the painting, hear the music, is impenetrable. It may even come towards us in a spirit of hermetic guardedness, of camouflage, of outright deception. *Trompe-l'œil* is an ontological, not merely a technical, possibility. It is the very force of declared intent, what Keats called "the palpable design upon us" in bad art, in *kitsch*, which we must learn to ignore. The promise of authorized, finally revealed meaning may be the Siren song. No such authorization, no such *auctoritas*, can be materially demonstrated. Would it not humiliate, make mute the freedom that meets freedom?

All this is so. And yet.

Though acts of reception and of understanding are in some measure fictions of ordered intuition, myths of reason, this truth does not justify the denial of intentional context. It is as absurd to discard as mendacious, as anarchically opaque, the bearing of contextual probability and suggestion, as it is to invest in such probability any blind trust. The negations of post-structuralism and of certain varieties of deconstruction are precisely as dogmatic, as political as were the positivist equations of archival historicism. The 'emptiness of meaning' postulate is no less *a priori*, no less a case of despotic reductionism than were, say, the axioms of economic and psycho-sociological causality in regard to the generation of meaning in literature and the arts in turn-of-the-century pragmatism and scientism.

Our encounter with the freedom of presence in another human being, our attempts to communicate with that freedom, will always entail approximation. So will our perceptions, our decipherments of articulate imagining. The point is obvious to anyone with even a rudimentary practice of calculus or the geometry of tangents. We advance step by step towards a delineation of the given space; our perceptions are more and more justly incident to the circumference of possible intent and meaning. The congruence is never complete. It is never uniform with its object. If it was, the act of reception would be wholly equivalent to that of original enunciation. Our guest would have nothing to bring us. But exactly as in differential calculus, the open-endedness of the philological method does not annul its rigour or revelatory potential. On the contrary. It is the very fact that circumscription and determination are only partial, that they remain mobile, self-correcting, which confirms both the autonomy of the meaningful presence in the poetic and the integrity of our reception. I have said before: a good reading falls short of the text or art object by a distance, by a perimeter of inadequacy which are themselves luminous as is the corona around the darkened sun. The falling-short is a guarantor of the experienced 'otherness' – the freedom to be or not to be, to enter into or abstain from a commerce of spirit with us – in the poem, the painting, the piece of music.

Also here, the naïve analogy with the stranger's entrance, with the modulation, where it is possible, of stranger into guest, instructs us. We bring what surrounding evidence, what precedent experience (which is culture), what instrumentalities of discernment we can, to bear on the possible meanings of this coming. We seek to make out the intelligibility, the claims upon us, of his gestures and discourse. We realize full well that our comprehension, even as it deepens into intimacy, most particularly where it deepens into intimacy, will remain partial, fragmentary, subject to error and to revaluation. But this knowledge does not induce us to presume that the presence before us is one of spectral vacancy or falsehood. Nor, and this is of utmost relevance, does it prompt us to strip it bare, to dissect it in some brutal rhetoric or hermeneutic of total penetration and subjection. Censorship anatomizes and makes naked. Commercialism domesticates, makes piece-work of, as on an assembly line, literature and the arts. There are elements of like violence, though seemingly playful, in structuralism and deconstruction. (Consider Roland Barthes's *S/Z*.)

Where there is *cortesia* between freedoms, a vital distance is kept. A certain reserve persists. Understanding is patiently won and, at all times, provisional. There are questions we do not ask of our 'caller', of the summoner's presence in the poem or the music, lest they diminish both the object of our questioning and ourselves. There are cardinal discretions in any fruitful encounter with the offering of form and of sense. Where it is most expressive, language, art, music makes sensible to us a root of secrecy within itself. The arc of metaphor, without which there can be neither shaped thought nor performative intelligibility, spans an undeclared foundation. Maturity of mind and of sensibility in the face of the aesthetic demands "negative capability" (Keats). It allows us to inhabit the tentative. Because 'the real thing' is held to be a fiction, a rhetorical trope and illusion with designs upon us, it is, in certain recent strategies of decompositional reading, to be pried open (there is an antinomian pathos in the impatient insistence on emptiness). The philological space, on the contrary, is that of the expectant, of the risks of trust taken in the decision to open a door.

How does this simile of entrance translate into our actual aesthetic experience? Where does it lead us?

It is indicative of the stylistic and intellectual climate now predominant, of the era of theory, that the personal phenomenality of the encounter with music, literature and the arts is left largely inarticulate. Current critical theory in its investigations of significant form finds almost nothing to say of the literal facts of our experience of the poem. What 'comes to pass' between the lives of the text or painting and our own? Even what is called 'Theory of Reception' remains primarily formal and historical in its review of successive stages of aesthetic interpretation.

There are motives for this analytic and descriptive avoidance of what is, palpably, the central issue. The histrionic bathos of much Romantic and post-Romantic testimony as to the sublimity or terror of the lyric, pictorial and musical experience, has left a dubious taste. We rightly suspect the eloquence of ardent response which characterizes a good deal of writing about literature and the arts from, say, Schiller and Shelley to Ruskin and Pater. Too many Muses and angelic presences (as in Rilke) have unfolded their lambent wings in too many lecture-emporia and *salons*. Rightly again, as I noted earlier, we no longer share the positivist and 'scientific' intimations of verifiable psychological data regarding the impact on us of musical, plastic or verbal statements. On a simply pragmatic level, we know that it requires tact, technical authority and control of a rare order to communicate to others, in some lucid and scrupulous way, the quality, the intelligible ramifications of an aesthetic experience, particularly where that experience touches on the inmost of one's being. Nietzsche on and 'against' Wagner; Proust face-to-face with Vermeer; Mandelstam reading Dante; Karl Barth labouring after Mozart: these are exemplary instances. In an almost unsettling sense, they constitute 'the art of art'. Such examples require introspective clarities and discretionary candours of the highest degree. To try and tell of what happens inside oneself as one affords vital welcome and habitation to the presences in art, music and literature is to risk the whole gamut of muddle and embarrassment. It is, if one is not oneself an artist, thinker or witness of condign strength, to lay oneself open to (often deserved) ridicule and rebuke where these hurt most. Springs are licensed to murmur and gush; not adults. The psychological and social fact that ours is an age in which embarrassment terrorizes even the confident and the lonely has sharpened the inhibitions. Structuralist semiotics and decon-struction are expressions of a culture and society which 'play it cool'.

These are potent rationalizations. At the close of this argument I want to suggest that they mask a more radical flinching; that the embarrassment we feel in bearing witness to the poetic, to the entrance into our lives of the mystery of otherness in art and in music, is of a metaphysical-religious kind. What I need to state plainly here is both the prevailing convention of avoidance, and my personal incapacity, both intellectual and expressive, to overcome it adequately. I am not of the company cited above. Yet the attempt at testimony must be made and the ridicule incurred. For what else are we talking about?

4

I want to delineate, as directly as I can, the characteristic immediacies of the 'happening to us' of created forms in poetics and the arts. These immediacies are familiar to anyone who has entered into personal relation with a poem, painting, piece of music at anything beyond the most trivial or casually enforced level. Yet they are very difficult to put into words.

That which comes *to call on us* – that idiom, we saw, connotes both spontaneous visitation and summons – will very often do so unbidden. Even where there is a readiness, as in the concert hall, in the museum, in the moment of chosen reading, the true entrance into us will not occur by an act of will. The process of penetration, of implantation, suggests a chemical bonding, involuntary and, very frequently, initially unnoticed. In a celebrated analogy, Coleridge invokes "hooked atoms" of mental association, of similitude and recollection. But the bonding between the aesthetic object and ourselves does seem to lie deeper than do mechanisms of association or remembrance, certainly on the cerebral, conscious plane. It points towards those unconscious or subconscious predispositions, towards those ingrained, unelected affinities between configurations of reception and of stimulus which the alchemists, in regard to elemental alliances, spoke of as 'sympathies'. The text, the musical structure, the picture or form, fulfil, in what may be, almost literally, a spatial sense, awaitings, needs we knew not of. We had been expecting that which we may well not have known to be, and to be complementary to us. The shock of correspondence – it can be muted and nearly indiscernibly gradual – is one of being possessed by that which one comes to possess. Keats gave that shock stylized expression when he told of first looking into Chapman's version of Homer. The entrance of the aesthetic motion of meaning into the psyche, of how it takes lodging in depth, is rendered famously in Proust's account of how "the little phrase" in Vinteuil's sonata is received by the narrator. But each and every one of us, however bounded our sensibility, will have known such unbidden, unexpected entrances by irrevocable guests. It was between trains, in a Frankfurt station bookstall, that I picked up and leafed through, scarcely attentive, a very thin book of poems, the rather odd name of whose author had caught the corner of my eye. Almost the first line I skimmed across or towards spoke of a language to be composed of words "north of the future". I do not now recall whether I caught the intended train, but Paul Celan has never left me.

How does the graft on to our being *take*? What is it that turns the momentary reception (the knock at the door) – even where that reception is involuntary, subliminal, adverse, for there are many images, tunes, evocations we would gladly be rid of – into tenancy? The honest answer is that we do not know. Both intuitively and theoretically, Western speculation on the psychology of aesthetic reception, from Plato to Freud and Jung, has been drawn towards intimations of *re*-cognition, of *déjà-vu* and *déjà-entendu*. We have met before.

There are two ways of approaching this profoundly suggestive but, until now, wholly undemonstrable conjecture (which is itself a dramatic parable, with its rhetoric of the primordial).

A slippage in our time-sense, a momentary superposition of past and present could generate a subconscious feel of recognition. What I would call a 'wobble' in our psychic co-ordinates of temporality creates an opening for, a 'hold' for and sensation of familiarity with, the poem, the painting or the melody. It appears more than plausible that external circumstances and internal dispositions in the moment in which the 'caller' comes to our threshold can provoke this 'wobble'. All of us have experienced twilit, penumbral moods of diffuse attention and unresistant receptivity on the one hand, and of tensed, heightened focus on the other. Sexual elements surely enter into our readiness or unreadiness for the aesthetic (to hear music, to take in a text with the beloved). Stimulants, narcotics, agents of reverie and of hallucination are known to crack the crust of self-possession, of walled self-sufficiency and, concomitantly, to enlarge synapses of reception. Romanticism, Surrealism, Futurism systematically cultivated such fissures opening into inward spaces of the psyche. During the transient eclipse of the ego, other presences find their luminous or shadowy way.

An even more speculative notion is conceivable. There may be in literature, music and the arts lineaments, spoors of a presentness prior to consciousness and to rationality as we know them. There may be vestiges of a pre-logical, certainly a pre-grammatical sedimentation of visual and auditory matter, of sequences (as in narrative and music). The inception of human consciousness, the genesis of awareness, must have entailed prolonged 'condensations' around intractable nodes of wonder and of terror, at the discriminations to be made between the self and the other, between being and non-being (the discovery of the scandal of death). Our modern dreams have long passed into grammatical, cultural modes, into a symbolic repertoire of a social kind. But the experience of the poetic, of the freedom of being made intelligible form, could communicate to us something of the incipience of human self-realization, of the first encounters with the self. The analogy I have in mind would be that of 'background radiation', of 'background noise' in which astrophysicists and cosmologists see tracers leading towards, and vestiges of, the origins of our universe.

The coming into perceptibility and, ultimately, intelligible shapes, of the rudiments of self may have been, in some manner we cannot reconstrue or paraphrase, musical. Music could have initiated the sensation, and later the controlled experience, of the multiple existence within time and space in the psyche of different levels of energy, of different and even conflicting currents of self-consciousness. Metaphor in language – the prime mover – and relations between chromatic values and spaces, which are the matter of the arts, would, thus, be an evolutionary modulation or translation into more semantic, representational codes of the arc of melody. The freedom and the constraints of key-relations, of rhythm in musical structures, could, when they take life inside us, be an immensely late marker, as is the light we receive from the outermost galaxies, of the ordering of the charged but disseminate particles which crystallized into humanized self-hood. Thus Verlaine's *"musique avant toute chose"* would have its secret truth.

Entering into us, the painting, the sonata, the poem brings us into reach of our own nativity of consciousness. It does so at a depth inaccessible in any other way. Literature and the arts are the perceptible witness to that freedom of coming into being of which history can give us no account. Hence the utterly arresting congruence between Aristotle's assertion in the *Poetics* that fiction is "truer and more universal than history" and Jung's inference of archetypes, of inherited figurations and narrative icons, at the roots of human consciousness. I find this congruence seductive. But there is, I repeat, no external evidence for it whatever. It may be pure fantastication. How, moreover, would it explain the sensations of homecoming brought to us by cheap music, by *kitsch*-art or by the shoddiest of jingles and romances?

Even as it comes unbidden, so the possessive grip of the work of art on our consciousness and recollection can be value-free. Obsessions can be, they often are, indiscriminate. Eros and the aesthetic experience are close kindred. The spell of form, the hauntingness of recognition, as these enter into our lives, can have a logic of accord, a 'fit' in respect of our own edges and needs, which can be independent of generalized, consensual quality. *Pace* the lacquered glitter of the market-place, ugly men and women, the lame and the dissolute, have their impassioned lovers. Cheap music, childish images, the vulgate in language, in its crassest sense, can penetrate to the deeps of our necessities and dreams. It can assert irrevocable tenure there. The opening bars, the hammer-beat *accelerando* of Edith Piaf's "*Je ne regrette rien*" – the text is infantile, the tune stentorious, and the politics which enlisted the song unattractive – tempt every nerve in me, touch the bone with a cold burn and draw me after into God knows what infidelities to reason, each time I hear the song, and hear it, uncalled for, recurrent inside me. Wagner raged at his inability to excise from within his remembrance and involuntary humming, the tin-pot tunes of a contemporary operetta, *The Postillion of Longjumeau*. There are rhymes, puns, jingle-effects flat as stale water, which mesmerize not only readers and listeners, but the greatest of poets (Will Shakespeare on *will*; Victor Hugo in hundredfold thrall to *ombre/sombre*). Yet other tunes, mental pictures, verbal sonorities and 'hook-ups', of equal catchiness and insistence, slip from notice and recollection. It is as if the honeycomb of each individual receptivity, of each individual psychic indwelling, were intricately specific. Though there are spatial contours and antennae which an individual shares with all other human beings, which he shares more directly with members of his historical situation, society and educational background, other 'cells' in his psyche are, as linguists would say, 'idiolectic'. They are patterned singularly to his own receptive and communicative internality. The chemistry of such formation escapes us. But the consequence, in regard to aesthetic response, to obsession, to elective affinity, is clear.

I would designate it by differentiating between a syllabus and a canon. We have seen how a syllabus is established over time. How it represents cultural, social, pedagogic choices which aim at a more or less stable consensus. We noted that the syllabus is instinct not only with aesthetic but also with political and political-economic motives and valuations. There is a politics in the marketing of the 'classical' as there is a counter-politics in the bartering of the subversive and the anarchic. A canon, on the contrary, is a profoundly personal construct. It may remain wholly private and unvoiced. It has its foundations in the ebb of the pre-conscious. It most probably originates in the, as yet, untautened weave of sensory shocks and rewards, of incipient accommodations to both an inner and an outer world, as these occur in the seminal phases of childhood. Adolescence, with its placement of sexuality within the person, is a primary moment of 'canonization', of the reception, selection for retention or rejection of the sensory and the significant in discourse, in music, in formal representation. Later ripeness and old age, in symmetrical contrast to childhood and to puberty, pare down the personal canon, discard from it all but the baggage judged indispensable towards evening. A canon is the guarded cata-logue of that in speech, music and art which houses inside us, which is irrevocably familiar to our homecomings. And this catalogue will include, if it is honestly arrived at and declared (even if solely to oneself), all manner of ephemeral, trivial, possibly mendacious matter. As in the rummage-room or Alad-din's attic. It is also the bad rhymester, the pedlar of facile images, the organ-grinder whose work is not only ineradicable from our memories, but continues to nourish, to quicken our innermost wants. No man or woman need justify his personal anthology, his canonic welcomes. Love does not argue its necessities.

It is the relations between syllabus and canon which are difficult to situate. There will be, within a given culture and inheritance of taste, much overlap. The masterpieces will tend to figure in one's personal and individual inventory. Whether they do so by virtue of authentic recognition or whether their authority of acceptance derives from external prestige, from pressures for conformity, from our sloth in the face of proclaimed values and laurels, is an awkward question. It touches on the grey, permeable boundaries between public and private, between convention and spontaneity, which mark all social and existential conditions. But there is, I believe, honest, individually realized congruence between "the best that is known and thought in the world", Matthew Arnold's perhaps too-confident designation of the touchstones of great art, literature, music on the one hand, and the intimate canon on the other. I shall try to state shortly, at the decisive turn in the argument, what I take to be the reasons for this concordance.

The point we have now reached is this: whatever its provenance, be it from the shared and public syllabus of excellence, be it from the private canon of chosen reception, or be it from both, the text, the work, the musical structure, has entered into us. We have given it, it has taken, 'the run of the house'. It has gained the freedom of our inner city. What follows?

Every human being who has experienced art, music, literature will have his or her own descriptive answer. Each account, each attempt at paraphrase or metaphoric approximation will prove inadequate in its own way. There is, in essence, common ground. But no individual telling of the possession by and possession of felt form and meaning quite translates into any other. It may be that there is no other domain of current human circumstance in which self-evident immediacy is so close to the inexplicable, in which Montaigne's explanation of the reasons for the foremost friendship, indeed love, in his life, "because he was he, because I was I", so marks the available limits of insight. We know, often with blinding obviousness, what it is we are trying to say about our relations or non-relations to the poem, the painting, the sonata. Yet we do not know either how to say it or, in any falsifiable, material sense, exactly what it is we are talking about.

The liberties taken by our 'tenant' vary almost boundlessly. They range from the barest flicker of momentary notice to the obsessive. The intensity, the lastingness of the aesthetic impact may, we noted, be wholly unrelated to the generally assigned quality or stature of its source. Accredited monumentalities pass us by; the ephemeral can be addictive. It is the sheer force of the experience, its insertion into the quick of our being, which challenge understanding and clear phrasing. Bottom's "translation", the close-woven bearing of that word as it applies to Bottom's consciousness, in *A Midsummer Night's Dream*, come as near as any presentment we have to the transformative powers of the aesthetic when they are at work in our identity and nature. Where the commerce between freedoms, where the liberties granted and taken are of integral strength, we are indeed "translated" (and the touch of enormity in regard to Bottom the Weaver is latent, always).

Dostoevsky's report of the effects on his sensibility, thought, on his sense of habitation in the world, of a Rubens *Descent from the Cross* which he encountered, unsolicited, in the Dresden art gallery, communicates the seismic tenor of that event. Ruskin on Turner is as near as we have to the minutes of a dialogue between an inrush of envisioned meaning, as turbulent, as demanding as are its technical-expressive means on the one hand, and an energized receptivity, a thinking eye and readiness of inner echo of the rarest discipline on the other. Ruskin's successive notations of his "Turner experience" are the chronicle of a shock both immediate and gradual (in the aesthetic, the deepest shocks of recognition unfold patiently out of immediacy). There are passages in Winckelmann, in Kenneth Clark's study of the nude, which press words into the accurate service of touch, which make of language a counterpart at only one remove to the tactile planes, incurvations, rounded warmths or intended chills of the marmoreal and the metallic. The best readers of texts, of architectural compositions (they are rare) can convey the genesis of their own sighting; they can suggest to us how the relevant organization and fabric come into conceptualized form within themselves and, correspondingly, within the observer's reception. The innervations which animate the work and those in the perceptive act ramify towards each other.

In so far as a man or woman is susceptible to *poiesis*, to meaning made form, he or she is open to incursions and appropriations by agencies of delight or of sadness, of assurance or of dread, of enlightenment or of perplexity, whose modes of operation are, finally, beyond paraphrase. This is a truism. Equally obvious, yet no more accessible to analysis, are the processes of transformation which the aesthetic sets in motion.

Our biological-somatic lineaments have scarcely changed over historical time, if at all. The art of the bison-painters of Lascaux is registered by precisely the same optic nerve and tactile empathy as the latest abstract painting. But it is art itself, it is our 'in-take' of it which, both in the social and the individual moment, modify the sensory. Metamorphosis comes of interaction. The re-orderings of visual codes of intelligible space in the gradual passage to perspective and the vanishing point in Western representational art is a classic (perennially contentious) case. The modulation of the image of the child, from miniature adult into live, autonomous unripeness, is another. As yet unavailable to Shakespeare, that modulation has been transformative in respect of theology – the Christ image – of familial life, of psychology. The complicated history of the self-portrait or, more precisely, of self-portrayal from the graffiti of craftsmen on medieval architraves to the self-mustering of a Giotto, of a Fra Angelico in the bystanders of a scriptural scene, from Rembrandt to Picasso, involves radical shifts and attempts at equilibrium in the identifications of what is carnal and what is spiritual, of what is public and what is private in the persona. Like Montaigne and Pascal, yet in a fundamentally different, iconic, way, Rembrandt's self-portraits and portraits of the old and the uncomely alter not only the sensory cognition of beauty – the economics of desire – but the demarcations between outward and inward areas of felt realness. Both sides of our skin are, as it were, made new.

The history of our vision of and feel for light has yet to be written. Even as there are doctrines of light in religious thought and mythology or in neo-Platonic philosophy, so there are, both implicitly and explicitly, in art. Our political awareness but also, if more subtly, our readings of the hours and the seasons, of wind and of water, are modified by the uses of light in the flat deeps of Piero della Francesca, by the light from Vermeer's casements, by Turner's lit storms, by the revolution that is Impressionism. Concomitantly, observe the mutations in the weight of darkness after Rembrandt's etchings, after Goya's 'black paintings' or Ad Reinhardt's *Black on Black*. It is no indulgent fantasy to say that poplars are on fire since Van Gogh or that aqueducts wear walking-shoes after Paul Klee.

The 'otherness' which enters into us makes us other.

Western tradition, both classical and Romantic, ascribes to the poetic in the stricter sense, that is to say to the forms of meaning within language, the highest aesthetic potency. It is the epic and the lyric, the tragedy and the comedy, it is the novel which exercises the most penetrative authority over our consciousness. It is via language that we are most markedly and enduringly 'translated'. This primacy appears to be grounded in the very centre of our humanity. There are, arguably, elements of graphic-semiotic ornament, there are, almost unquestionably, modes of musical utterance and mimesis, of choreographic movement, which man shares with his animal kindred. The construct of the verbal is, so far as we know, uniquely and essentially human.

This generic singularity has given to our civilization and to its transmission a profoundly textual character. It is in sacred texts, in laws, in literature that civilization is housed. The relations between the sacred and the legally or ethically prescriptive ('the worded') on the one hand, and the poetic or fictive on the other, have always been vexed. What matters is that literary invention should be regarded, be it with welcome or with mistrust (both attitudes are paradigmatic in Plato), as one of the foundational triad. In the poem, in the prayer, in the law, the reach of words is made very nearly equivalent to the humanity in man.

This estimate is so ubiquitous to us, the 'letter' so palpably inhabits 'literacy', that dissent or questioning are rare. There must be, there assuredly are, men and women of evident sensibility and answerability of spirit for whom Titian, say, or Rodin represent as transformative, as possessing a presence as Homer or Dante or Shakespeare. There are disciplines of perception, in both East and West, for whom configurations of formed objects in open or closed spaces – the garden, the seemingly empty Japanese room – communicate a density of articulate repose, an eloquence of abstention, surpassing any experienced in reading a text. The issue of the ultimate power of music over mortal understanding, this is to say over the understanding of mortality, is one I want to return to.

Given these reservations, it is, none the less, patent that discussions of the emotive and intellectual impact of the aesthetic have set at their pivot the word, spoken and written. It is this very fact which so inhibits any confident findings. How are words to systematize, to externalize, the effect of words? What grammatology, what treatise on poetics and rhetoric can hope to convey, save by the use of *figura* and metaphor (which is, perhaps, to say, by inspired gossip), the grammar of the overwhelming?

The foremost witness is that of the child. The open door which the child proffers to the day and night visitants out of the imaginary is one of pristine psychological truth. The room is, as yet, largely unfurnished. Wardrobes stand open to unicorns. Consolers and felonious shades can enter and move about at liberty. The story told to a child, the tale read, the ballad committed, perhaps unawares, to memory, are taken to heart. Literally. In most adults, this immediacy tends to diminish. The entrances and alarms of the fictive run up against the cluttered, cautionary domesticities of rationalized, disenchanted response. It is in intimate commerce with the vitality and substance of his imagined callers that a child tests and assembles his components of the nascent self. And 'callers' or 'summoners' is the correct term. The child follows after: to Crusoe's island or Gulliver's archipelago, to Middle Earth and galactic wars. He is initiated to delight as well as to fear. When there is night in the house or, as masters of whispering such as Walter de la Mare know, when noon is too still, fictions will introduce the child to the magnetism of menace.

To starve a child of the spell of the story, of the canter of the poem, oral or written, is a kind of living burial. It is to immure him in emptiness. Mythology, the voyages through Scylla and Charybdis, down rabbit holes, the turbulent logic of the biblical, the 'gardens of verse', are the great summoners. A comic-book is better than nothing so long as there is in it the multiplying life of language. The child must be made accessible, vulnerable to the springs of being in the poetic. There are risks. His visitants can turn ugly or hypnotic. There are adult men and women whose sensibility has not outgrown, has not ironized into self-awareness, childhood charades of mythical heroism or fantasies of the despotic. The nursery tale, the pathos of stuffed and furry things, can translate damagingly into later needs. The shock of the revelatory fable, often misconstrued, can lame mature sexuality. But such risks must be run. If the child is left empty of texts, in the fullest sense of that term, he will suffer an early death of the heart and of the imagination. I do underline 'in the fullest sense'. The waking of human freedom can also occur in the presence of pictures, of music. It is, in essence, a waking through the pulse of narrative as it beats in aesthetic form. But it does seem to be words that rap most surely at the door. Did God, asks Jewish folklore, not invent man so that He might hear him tell tales?

Receptivities are as individual as snow crystals. There are those who flinch from the untruth of fiction. There can be colour-blindness, tone-deafness or some impatience, almost organic, at the seeming irresponsibility of the fabled (this impatience is urgent in Plato, in certain Church Fathers, in Dickens's Mr Gradgrind). In other men and women, on the contrary, the obsessiveness, the claims of the imaginary can be so exigent as to induce a certain loss of 'the reality principle'. There is no carapace supple or strong enough to filter out the contagion of textual enormity (there are stretches of slow torture in *Othello* I can face only rarely and of which I instinctively make remembrance inaccurate). We have seen how the sensory weight of the dream or the terrors of the fictive can blank out the cry in the street. Thus there is in the concentrate of language we call 'literature', as in the compactions of art and of music, a most potent insinuation of unworldliness. Filled, possessed by the dynamics of the melody, by the *personae* of the play or the novel, we may find daylight and truth-functions vacuous. Shelley pronounced that no man who had met with Sophocles' Antigone could ever again give to a living woman the full weight of his love, of his desiring trust. In the economy of the soul, whose means are not without bounds, a central niche has been pre-empted and a jealous radiance entrenched.

Here the matter of pornography has its pertinence. The cant put forward on this topic is often as nauseating as the thing itself. The plain fact is that pornographic art and writing, notably of the sadistic kind – and there is sadism in *all* pornography precisely to the degree that sexuality is objectified, that the human body or some part thereof is made the object of libidinal waste and servitude – will seize upon the echo-surfaces, upon the agencies of mimetic hunger in the psyche. Where this hunger is merely one for superfluity, where competing and corrective stimuli and satisfactions lie to hand – this seizure is short-lived. It will produce the fundamentally trivial, though powerful, facsimile text of masturbation. But let this seizure come upon emptiness, upon deprivation (social, economic, cultural), let the fantasy be an exclusive promise of the fact, and the consequences can be those of destructive and self-destructive re-enactment.

The problem of censorship in regard to the dissemination, textual and graphic, of the pornographic-sadistic is one of constant difficulty. But it is not this I want to debate: it is the seminal, illustrative function of the fictive within any argument on poetics. As Dante teaches, words can, in some substantive sense, make the soul hot to the touch of love. Literalism, the documentary, seek escape from the charring authority of fiction. Because it is the fiction which takes hold. Books burn long before and after they are burnt. Censors, book-burners, pornographers bear corrupt but unmistakable witness to the ambiguous mastery of texts over life. The effects are those of a chain reaction, much as high-energy physics recounts them. The verbal suggestion, the image or tonal associations released by aesthetic forms, in turn, generate further sequences of analogous, of answering, of variant formulation within us. Dormant wants are given a habitation and a name. The script of imitative possibility unfolds. A radical verity underlies, underwrites Sade's crazed prolixity. Written out, sexuality, the phantasms of exploitation and enslavement which continue to shadow our fragile schooling in humanity are unpunctuated. There can be no full stop to them. In an area whose genesis and structure are inaccessible to analysis, the nerve of sexuality and that of language are close-bound. The power over consciousness of the pornographic and the sadistic, of the literatures and graphics of hatred, is the exact and symmetrical parody of the power over consciousness of the discourse of love.

It is that discourse in which the encounter with 'the other' takes us to the edge, at once remote and very near, of an understanding of or a failing to understand, the very nature of the poetic. Plato's *Symposium*, St Augustine on discourse and dreams, Dante's *Vita Nuova*, Shakespeare's *Sonnets* and Joyce on the epiphanies of desire are of the essence. But the relations of Eros to *Logos* and the cardinal function of this relation in the creation and reception of art, poetry, music, cannot be made the object of systematic rationality. Here, again, there is the paradox of the interactions between what is most intimate, most singular to ourselves, and the mastering ingress of the aesthetic or, indeed, of the formulaic. Who but the rarest among us has made love new?

The words, phrases, tropes, gestures of spirit and body with which we seek to communicate the birth, ripening, withering of love in our being, with which we seek to convey these elemental experiences both to our own perception and to 'the other', whose otherness is, at this very point, most critical to us, are taken very largely, whether consciously or not, from the repertoire of the great sayers, painters, music-makers before us. In pre- or sub-literate European communities, well into the eighteenth century, the public scrivener offered his amorous client a choice of ready-made phrasings of intimacy, of passionate longing or ecstatic acceptance. The lover chose according to his means; today, telegrams of wooing or felicitation can still be composed according to set tags. But this formulaic visibility of the discourse of love stands for a much larger truth. According to the levels of our verbal and literate holdings, we experience and signify love as did Jack and Jill, as did Romeo and Juliet or Tolstoy's Natasha before us. Our jealousies ape Othello's. Lear is our 'stand-in' – an idiom which, itself, seeks out the cultural centrality of the mimetic, of the pre-figured – when our children visit us in silence or retribution. The broken syllables which generations whispered or panted in the rhetoric of seduction and of inter-course were out of Petrarch's phrase book.

Basic shifts are rare. But modernity has altered the lines dividing articulate transgression, taboos and the illicit from what is socially sanctioned in the speech and imaging of Eros. The areas assigned to the public and the private parts have been re-defined after *Madame Bovary*. The live ballast of privacy, of the unspoken, or of that spoken to the beloved in the unguarded nakedness of final trust is now exhibited. As never before, we are, even in the fumbling idiosyncrasies of our sexuality, pre-scripted, spoken for. The innocence of obscenity has moved into the last total embarrassment available to us, which is that of prayer. We know this if only by virtue of a supreme word-play and finding at the climax of one of Celan's late poems. He says to, he says of the beloved that she "beds and prays him free". The pun does not translate: *bettest/betest*. But the wonder of congruence is plain. The commerce of love finds the as-yet unspoken. Privacy is made new, Eros translates (as in Bottom) into *Logos*. And this translation speaks freedom.

It takes uncanny strength and abstention from *re*-cognition, from implicit *re*-ference, to read the world and not the text of the world as it has been previously encoded for us (the sciences know of this bind). The exceptional artist or thinker reads being anew. We Sunday-walkers come in the wake of Rousseau. There are nymphets at our street corners since Nabokov's *Lolita*. Nor is this scripting and pre-figuration by the imaginary a dominant fact of only those civilizations we regard as technically literate. The hold of oral narrative, of inherited fictions over so-called 'primitive' or illiterate societies is even stronger. Such societies can almost be defined as communities of authorized remem-brance, of ritual pre-scription. Because we are language and image animals, and because the inception and transmission of the fictive (the mythical) is organic to language, much, perhaps the major portion, of our personal and social existence is already bespoken. And those who speak us are the poets.

'It is the singer', anthropologists would say. And we know of no cultures where the poet and the singer are not, at the outset, the same. Intuitively, the song is held to have come first. The metrics of the poem, the cadences of our prose, are translations out of music. The universality of music, we have said, declares man's humanity. It extends from the signifying pitch or rudimentary cry to what I take to be the single most intricate organization of the interactions of feelings and of meanings known to us, which is that deployed in a string quartet. In turn, our perceptions, the immediacy of our perceptions of harmony and of discord would seem to correspond not only to our readings of inner states of personal being, but also to that of the social contract and, ultimately, of the cosmos (that 'music of the spheres'). The energy that is music puts us in felt relation to the energy that is life; it puts us in a relation of experienced immediacy with the abstractly and verbally inexpressible but wholly palpable, primary fact of being. The translation of music into meaning, into meaning that is entirely musical, carries with it what somatic and spiritual cognizance we can have of the core-mystery (how else is one to put it?) that we are. And that this energy of existence lies deeper than any biological or psychological determination. Thus we do seem to harbour at the threshold of the unconscious, at depths precisely unrecapturable by speech and the logic of speech, intimations, incisions in the synapses of sensibility, of a close kinship between the beginnings of music and those of humanly-enacted meaning itself. A world without music is, strictly considered, outside our persuasions of order and desire. It need not be a dead world in the geological or biological sense. But it would be explicitly inhuman.

Here, as well, the canonic insights are very few. Again, they include Plato and St Augustine. There are wonders of simile and invocation in Shakespeare; there are pages in Schopenhauer, in Nietzsche. We know of music as we know the spark and pressure at the centre of our own selves (or, perhaps, as we know of our own sleep). But we have no defining, systematic grasp of its constant, enormous impact. We can say that music is time organized, which means 'made organic'. We can say that this act of organization is one of essential freedom, that it liberates us from the enforcing beat of biological and physical-mathematical clocks. The time which music 'takes', and which it gives as we perform or experience it, is the only *free time* granted us prior to death. We can speculate, and have done so from the ancient rhapsodes to the neurophysiologists of today, on possible concordances – themselves a musical borrowing – between bodily rhythms and subliminal cadences on the one hand, and the structural conventions of music on the other. But where it is not metaphor, almost everything said remains, in a chasteningly etymological sense, verbiage.

What we know is the relevant power. Folktale and metaphysics, myth and psychotherapy, Eros and religious rites, share the knowledge that music can literally madden, that it can make violence vibrant, that it can console, exalt, heal, that it can wake Lear out of crazed blackness. There are cadences, chords, modulations which break or mend the heart, or, indeed, mend it in the breaking. There are tone-relations which make us strangers to ourselves or, on the contrary, impel us homeward. There are *andantes* (Mahler's trick of transcendence) which seem to break open the prison house of the ego and to make us one with the tidal peace of being. There are *scherzos* (too many in Mozart) in which laughter is perfectly real and, at the same time, where laughter is a last, unconquerable sadness. Melodies – I have cited the conviction that they are "the supreme mystery of man" – can arch across an abyss or they can, as it were, pulse underground, unsettling all foundations. All these, however, are lame banalities.

Where we try to speak of music, to speak music, language has us, resentfully, by the throat. This I believe to be the buried meaning of the fable of the Sirens. More ancient than language possessed of "thrones, dominions, powers", more secret than those bestowed on speech, music lies in wait for the speaker, for the logician, for the confidant of reason (Odysseus *par excellence*). The Sirens promise orders of understanding, of peace (harmonies) which transcend language. The language-animal, man, armoured in his will to power which is grammar and logic, must resist. He must deafen himself to the solicitations of the song. Otherwise he will be drawn out of himself – the ecstatic motion – to some irremediable sleep of reason.

But the Sirens are perennial. They are not destroyed by Odysseus' ruse. Behind the veil of rational discourse, music seems to hum and bruit. Sound is always threatening to pull after it, with the force of the ebbing tide, the servile stabilities of sense. It does so in every pun, in the rush and eddies of word-associations. Great poetry is, very exactly, that in which this homeward soughing of the musical tide is made to enrich, to deepen, the life of the word. A true poem, a live prose, a philosophic movement wholly consonant to its syntax, is one in which Odysseus sets observant words to the Sirens' song.

How music possesses us is a question to which we know no credible, let alone materially examinable answer. All we have are further images. And the defiant self-evidence of human experience.

Here lies easy prey for both positivism and deconstruction.

I have tried to say that the only account we can give of the ontological encounter between freedoms, as it takes place in our meeting with the aesthetic, is an intuitive one. The summary pointers I have given to the entrances into our consciousness and answering humanity of art, music and literature are impressionistic and metaphoric. They postulate an irreducible subjectivity, the finality of a self whose freedom, whose *cortesia*, make possible the recognition of the other. An axiom of dialogue underwrites the very concept of an encounter with intelligible form. Current epistemology and certain directions in psychology

– the lines of denial which lead from elements in Nietzsche to Lacan and Foucault – proclaim the vacancy of the subject. The ego, a fiction so useful to the atavistic pretensions and power-practices of so-called classical humanism, is dissolved. In turn, deconstruction negates any stability or plenitude of sense within enunciatory acts and forms.

I have underlined the radical edge, the suggestive virtuosity of these dissolutions and negations. Nothing I have said in the way of existential description, no recourse I have had to the immediacies and self-evidence of our common experience of meaning and of art, has *refuted*, logically, verifiably, the challenges of nihilism (where 'nihilism' is not pejorative, where it tells of the subversive provocations of the satyr-play). What is worse: my constant enlistment of images, similes, metaphors or ostensible examples of the most shop-worn kind reinforces the sceptical (the positivist) and the deconstructive case. Yet there can be no systematic, measurable model (theory) of the categories of possession and response which I have invoked. It is just the emotive fictions, the postulates of immediacy and of pathos which humanism has insinuated into grammar and into the sloth we call 'common sense', which the dialecticians of denial after Nietzsche and after Freud have set out to lay bare and to evacuate.

Let me reiterate a previous conclusion: on the secular level, on that of pragmatic psychology or of general consensus, the claims of nothingness cannot be adequately answered. If the terms of the argument are solely those of immanence, the free, real presence of meaning within form cannot be adequately defined or given metaphysical plausibility. Today, the liberal imagination is more or less at ease with the manifold discourse of uncertainties. It perceives in this multiplicity and indeterminacy of possible discourses and metaphoric modellings a guarantor of tolerance. It suspects in any thirst for absolutes not only an infantile simplicity but the old, cruel demons of dogma.

The relaxed ironies and liberalities of this position are attractive. At the same time, it may well be that they inhibit not only a deeper, more vulnerable access to the matter of the generation of meaning and of form, but that they are, themselves, the reflection of a certain reduced condition of the poetic and of the act of creation in our culture (what I have called 'the epilogue'). It is these propositions I want to test. This entails taking one further step, a step beyond both moral good sense and the existentially empirical. It is a step embarrassing *beyond words* where 'embarrassment' must serve precisely as that which compels inference beyond words. Transcendence is another, almost technical, name for that passage. Dante is of help when he tells of "turning the bow (*la poppa*) towards morning". To do so may cause a *folle volo*, "a foolish, an insensate flight". But I see no other.

5

Why should there be art, why poetic creation? The question is an exact analogue to that posed by Leibniz: why should there be being and substance, why should there not be nothing? But it is a more restricted question. The teeming prodigality of the phenomenal world, its inexhaustible deployment ('thereness') of sensory, communicative energies and forms is such as to saturate even the hungriest appetite for perception, even the most ample capacities for reception. The colours, metamorphic shapes and sonorities of the actual exceed immeasurably human capacities for registration and response. The animate logic of congruent symmetries, of organic motifs in the human body, is of a designate wonder – a wonder of design as we see it in

Leonardo's famous icon of frontal and cosmic man – such as to overwhelm understanding. And it is in this tensed caesura between analytic intelligibility and perception, when cognition holds its breath, that our sense of being is host to beauty. Why, then, art, why the created realm of fiction?

Compelled to take the guise of a verbal proposition, of an abstract claim, no reply can be adequate to match the force of the obvious. I can only put it this way (and every true poem, piece of music or painting says it better): there is aesthetic creation because there is *creation*. There is formal construction because we have been made form. Today, mathematical models proclaim access to the origins of the present universe. Molecular biology may have in reach an unravelling of the thread whose beginning is that of life. Nothing in these prodigious conjectures disarms, let alone elucidates, the fact that the world is when it might not have been, the fact that we are in it when we might, when we could not have been. The core of our human identity is nothing more or less than the fitful apprehension of the radically inexplicable presence, facticity and perceptible substantiality of the created. It is; we are. This is the rudimentary grammar of the unfathomable.

I take the aesthetic act, the conceiving and bringing into being of that which, very precisely, could not have been conceived or brought into being, to be an *imitatio*, a replication on its own scale, of the inaccessible first *fiat* (the 'Big Bang' of the new cosmologies, before which there cannot be, in true Augustinian fashion, any 'time', is no less a construed imperative and 'boundary-condition' than is the narrative of creation in religion). The conceptually intractable nature of that primal 'let there be' entails the possibility, itself conceptually inaccessible except in a trivially formal sense, of preceding nothingness, of the void. Even the most innovative, revolutionary text, canvas, tonal composition, arises from something: from the limits of physiology, from the potential of the linguistic or material means, from social-historical ambience. Deep inside every 'art-act' lies the dream of an absolute leap out of nothingness, of the invention of an enunciatory shape so new, so singular to its begetter, that it would, literally, leave the previous world behind. But the writing of poems, the making of music, the carving of stone or wood by mortal men and women is not only grounded in available circumstance: it is a *fiat*, a creative motion, always after the first. It is the nature of that 'posteriority' – the term and the question are already vital in Aristotle – which demands clarification.

Traditionally, the philosophy and psychology of art have provided a ready answer. Whatever its seeming novelty, whatever its techniques of dislocation, the verbal fiction, the painting, the sculpture, are ultimately mimetic. Surrealism, collages, non-representational tactics in word or form are merely disguises. The elements of the world, of the components of inhabited existentiality, are there. A 'black on black' is a snapshot of the night; a Centaur is a hyphen between manifest realities. The obstinate 'thereness' of things (this is the very theme of the crucial poetry of Ponge), the inference of immanence, seek out even the most extreme of verbal fantastications. Whether we would or not – and this constitutes the unbounded prison-house of language – our thinking eye construes shadows of familiarity, of signifying sequence, out of nonsense verse, out of concrete writing and apparently random play. Some finality of realism, of socially sanctioned reproduction, is, so far as literature and the plastic arts go, not so much a free option as it is an inescapable fact.

The category of the mimetic does, since Aristotle, account for the eminent sum of that which we experience as literature and the arts. We read poems and novels, we look at paintings, because they are, though often in a disconcertingly oblique or masked vein, of and about the world. That dependent indwelling, that 'aboutness', even where the mirrors are tricked, does, in the final analysis, solicit and satisfy some profound impulse towards recognition. As Aristotelian doctrine has it, the human animal imitates, it is instinct with re-enactment.

We note at once that the mimetic principle applies only to the more trivial, programmatic modes of music. What, in the world, is like music? What is music like? I will again be pressing the question at the close of this essay. The feebleness of our verbal answers to it seems to me of the utmost illumination.

But even in respect of the ontologically narrative forms, which are those of the poetic and the artistic in the narrower sense, the mimetic concept, the instinctual *imitatio mundi*, leaves too much unanswered. Given the world, why the second-hand of fiction, of the arts? If *mimesis* is the necessary and sufficient power, why, then, should reproductive fidelity not be the summit of aesthetic merit? Why should not all formal invention aspire to the condition of photographic innocence? There are, to be sure, programmatic-political codes of *verismo*, of 'social realism' which, in fact, seek to dictate this aspiration. The free imagination holds them in contempt. If invocations of innate mimesis do go a long way towards the 'how' of literature and of the arts, they do not tell us, except in a deterministically psychological sense, of the 'why'. Again, I ask: why should there be poems (Leibniz would ask: why should there not be no poems)? The axiom that there is *poiesis* 'because' there is creation is, presumably, commonplace. But it is that 'because' which challenges understanding.

I believe that the making into being by the poet, artist and, in a way yet to be defined, by the composer, is *counter*-creation.

The pulse of motive which relates the begetting of meaningful forms to the first act of creation, to the coming into being of being (German *Schöpfung* has, within it, both nascence and the fertile abyss), is not mimetic in any neutral or obeissant sense. It is radically agonistic. It is rival. In all substantive art-acts there beats an angry gaiety. The source is that of loving rage. The human maker rages at his coming *after*, at being, forever, second to the original and originating mystery of the forming of form. The more intense, the more maturely considered the fiction, the painting, the architectural project, the more palpable inside it will be the tranquil fury of secondarity. The more sensible will be the master maker's thrust towards a rivalling totality. The mortal artist would beget – that "only begetter" at the inception of Shakespeare's Sonnets – he would encompass, he would make an articulate *summa* of the world, as the unnamable rival, the "other craftsman" (Picasso's expression) did in those six days. The most concise of *haikus*, the briefest of Webern's studies, an early Kandinsky of a rider in a nightwood, so concentrated in scale that we must bend close, can do just that. They create a counter-world so entire, so imprinted with the mark of their craftsman's hand, his 'second-hand', that this world will "rap and knock and enter in our soul" (Browning) and that we in turn give it echo, sanctuary of remembrance, by discovering in it a habitation for our most intimate needs and recognitions.

True, the means of the artist's and poet's counter-construction, of his *mundus contra mundum*, are, more often than not, those of the extant (again, music is the central outsider). Even a Dante cannot fully realize his ardent desire to say *quello che mai fue detto d'alcuna*, "that which was never said by anyone". Even a Van Gogh cannot, altogether, 'make it new'. Fictions and formal imaginings do select, recombine from among the world's warehouse. A harvest is a gathering. But they do so in what I want to define as a high, constant *invidia*, a pious or incensed envy. The major text, the portrait, but also the landscape and still-life ask: 'Why was I not in at the beginning, why is not mine the organizing deed of form coming into meaning?' All nomination – and the poets, the artists are those who give names to the shapes and presences of being – contains its grain of violence, its wrestling for primacy. The image of Jacob and his Angel is, above all others, emblematic of the poetic. 'Why was I named before I could name, why must I limp after?' asks the poet.

Hence the pivotal place of self-portrayal in *poiesis*. It is the autobiographical motif, the self-portrait which is the least imitative, the least mirroring of aesthetic constructs. 'Painting himself', a charged phrase, the writer or artist re-enacts the creation of his own persona. He had not willed that creation; he had no choice in its lineaments. The self-portrait is the expression of his compulsion to freedom, of his agonistic attempt to repossess, to achieve mastery over the forms and meanings of his own being. There is hardly a more imperious act of 'second' creation, nowhere are more drastic challenges posed to one's unmastered coming into being, than in the sequence of Rembrandt's self-portraits. Here, materially, the maker of man is man. Where do we find a more mordant insurgence against the 'other shaper' than in the last self-portraits of Van Gogh, most notably that of the artist in his blue smock, holding in his hand those props of counter-creation which are his palette and brushes? There is in that canvas a nearing of death, but of death held momentarily at bay because it is looked at with a specific freedom. A kindred freedom, the mortal artisan's compulsion to create for himself and others the singularity, the verity of his own essence in the face both of the servitude of his unwilled, unchosen coming into the world, and in the face of the absurd,

205

unnaming logic of death, inspires Shostakovich's fifteen Quartets. Here autobiography is an inadequate rubric. These quartets constitute, in a sense discarded by modern biology, an act of spontaneous generation. The composer 'composes' his own private, social, political identity. He is re-born to an inviolate freedom, to a possession of his own coming and going hither. The power, the intricacy of counter-creation in Shakespeare's Sonnets (as in Michelangelo's) is manifold. Matchless in his capacity to people the world anew throughout his plays, Shakespeare, in the Sonnets, deliberately invokes the presence of a rival master. Scholarship would identify some contemporary playwright or poet. And there may be that component. But the inference cuts much deeper. The contest is that between maker and maker. Did the primal architect beget the only begetter? In their pressure of introspection, in their inexhaustible modulations on rivalry, on birth, a pressure and a modulation at once delicate and strangely violent, the Sonnets would re-appropriate, would tease out of unwilled mystery, the true nature, the created and creative identity of Shakespeare himself. Here again, self-portraiture is the most adversarial mode of creation. Mimesis is repossession.

In stating this hypothesis, I am wholly conscious of its possible bias towards maleness. I fully sense its more than metaphoric inference both of a masculine primacy in the creation of great fictive forms – a primacy not altogether explicable on social, historical or economic grounds – and of a patriarchal, militant image or metaphor of God. There is, possibly, though by no means necessarily, a gender-bias in any model of creation as agonistic, as an act of wrestling with, against the 'other maker'. I am convinced that there is in the poetry, in the novels written by women, as compelling a force of counter-creation, of life-giving repossession and *corrigenda* of the world as in those written by men. Have there been greater wrestlers with the "Angel which is terrible" than, say, George Eliot or Akhmatova? And yet. Is there in the almost total absence from drama of any major woman writer some formidable hint? Is the biological capacity for procreation, for engendering formed life which is cardinal to woman, in some way, at some level absolutely primordial to a woman's being, so creative, so fulfilling, as to subvert, as to render comparatively pallid, the begetting of fictive personae which is the matter of drama and of so much representative art? Could a woman's experience of the birth of her child – an experience quintessentially inaccessible to male perception – be so immediate in its kinship with the enigma, with the holiness of the being of life itself ("why is there not nothing?"), that it all but rules out the impulse to rivalry with a 'jealous God' which seems to me so crucial to the aesthetic? The often legitimate rancour of current feminist critiques, the vengeful impatience of the feminist indictment of traditional aesthetic and philosophic theory, are such as to make inquiry difficult. The mere platitude that literature, the arts and, above all, musical composition have been, until now, overwhelmingly of a male provenance provokes a bitter refusal of discussion. The conjecture – I have hinted at it already – that this fact has roots other than 'phallocratic' oppression, social constraint or domestic servitude, is held to be inadmissible. The pity of it. For there is, I venture to believe, no issue more pertinent – albeit intractably complex and resistant to psychological or sociological positivism – than that of gender and poetics, of gender, of sexuality and of the impulse to fiction. Can we honestly think further about creation and genesis, about the bringing into being of life-forms which relate the poem or the painting to existentiality itself, if we do not consider the essence of form-giving that is child-birth and the abstinence from *poiesis* which this act may entail? Do women their "ripe thoughts" in their "brain inhearse,/Making their tomb the womb wherein they grew"? I, most assuredly, do not know the answer. Perhaps Robert Frost did when he spoke of "counter-love".

What is certain is that the great artificers, and they *are* essentially men, have made no secret of their wrestling. Michelangelo's Sonnets seem to mark the rounds of those fierce bouts. The promise of the figure is alive inside the stone. Only Michelangelo's "rude hammer" can force it to the light out of its immemorial hiddenness, out of the secret sleep of matter. But is he, then, its maker? Incessantly, the master struggles with the source of prefiguration, and in that struggle the jealousy and the piety are one. The conceit, in both the common and the technical sense, of the poet, of the artist, of Mozart or of Beethoven as *alter deus*, has its remote ancestry in the near-divinization of Homer, in the sentiment, pervasive among the neo-Platonists, among the pedagogues and grammarian-critics of late antiquity, that the *Iliad* and the *Odyssey* did represent a more than human feat of ordering creation. Had not Hesiod and Homer, according to Herodotus, been responsible for the initial nomination and qualification as to their respective powers and labours, of the very gods? In turn, did one not open Virgil's *Aeneid* at random so as to discover in the found passage a numinous guide to, a revelation of, one's own destiny (the *sortes*)?

The poet, the master craftsman as 'another god' is a Renaissance commonplace. It runs like a bright thread, at once hubristic and pious, through Cellini's memoirs and informs, uncannily, his great carving of Christ on the Cross now in the Escorial. This motif of alternate divinity may well be the decisive clue towards the mania of invention and design in Leonardo, towards the unmistakable paradigm of the likeness of God the Father in

Leonardo's self-portraiture. In his preface to an exhibition catalogue of Gauguin (1895), Strindberg is acerbic: Gauguin is "the Titan who envies the Creator and in his spare time makes his own little Creation". A Creation, one would add, obsessively Edenic, almost vehemently intent on a cancellation of the Fall. Striking is the force and persistence of the *topos* of the artist as god, of God the rival, in an age reputedly secular. "God is in reality nothing but another artist" (*otro artista*) declared Picasso whose own appetite for invention, for self-recreation was, indeed, that of a demiurge. Having completed his paintings in the Chapel of the Rosary at Vence, Matisse ruled: "I did it for myself." "But you told me you were doing it for God," objected Sister Jacques-Marie. Matisse: "Yes, but I am God." James Joyce's simile for the playwright in *A Portrait of the Artist as a Young Man* has its shop-worn pride and disaffection: "The artist, like the God of creation, remains within or behind or beyond or above his handiwork, invisible, refined out of existence, indifferent, paring his fingernails." The statements are legion. And they are being made today.

We readers, listeners, viewers, experience the aesthetic, answer to the testing freedom of its ingress into our being, by coming to recognize within its formalities the lineaments of creation itself. Responding to the poem, to the piece of music, to the painting, we re-enact, within the limits of our own lesser creativity, the two defining motions of our existential presence in the world: that of the coming into being where nothing was, where nothing could have continued to be, and that of the enormity of death. But, be it solely on a millennial scale, the latter absolute is attenuated by the potential of survivance in art. The lyric, the painting, the sonata endure beyond the life-span of the maker and our own. It is the aesthetic which, past any other mode accessible to us, is the felt configuration of a negation (however partial, however 'figurative' in the precise sense) of mortality. Imaging to ourselves the fictive situation or personae in the text, recomposing perceptually the objects or visage in the painting, making audition resonant to the music via an inner complementarity, at once conceptual and bodily, we remake the making. To read well, to take in the light of specific presentness in the painting, to hear the dynamic relations in the tonal argument, is to generate anew, to wake out of silence, out of potential absence, the proceedings of the artist. An aesthetic theory is always an attempt to bring to bear on the joyous, libertarian scandal of resurrection the concept of historical and rational form.

We have seen that even the most penetrative, concordant response will encounter an irreducible 'otherness'. No reading finally encompasses the meanings, the life-in-meaning, of the poem. Where it is worth serious joy and welcome, an aesthetic form, a counter-creation, contains that which defies definite, stable incorporation. When artists and writers tell us that they are not regents over the complete or latent meanings of their own devisings, it is to this 'otherness' that they testify. When readers, interpreters or viewers of comparable sensibility and knowledge offer discordant responses to the same work, it is simply that their own free being has come up against differing facets of that in the aesthetic form which is itself irreducible to that form. This 'otherness' seems to me to be, almost materially, like an ever-renewed vestige of the original, never wholly accessible moment of creation. It is, in the idiom and image of current cosmology, the 'background radiation' which tells of the coming into being of our world. But unlike these spectral wavelengths, the 'otherness' which both maker and receiver experience in poetics, in music, in the arts, has not only a specific gravity – it is the unyielding self-concealment, the freedom to be silent in that which we love and hope to know best – but, often, an aura of terror. Hence, so famously, Rilke's cry to the 'Angels', to those who break him open at the beginning of the *Duino Elegies*. All departures, all beginnings out of the peace of nothingness, are fearful.

In most cultures, in the witness borne to poetry and art until most recent modernity, the source of 'otherness' has been actualized or metaphorized as transcendent. It has been invoked as divine, as magical, as daimonic. It is a presence of radiant opacity. That presence is the source of powers, of significations in the text, in the work, neither consciously willed nor consciously understood. It is, today, conventional to ascribe this vital excess to the unconscious. Such ascription is a secular phrasing of what I have called 'alterity'. The trope of the unconscious, however we seek to locate its empirical validity, is a translation into a seemingly rational code of that which earlier vocabularies and thought-systems referred to as the *daimon*, as the mantic breath of strangeness which speaks through the rhapsode, which guides the sculptor's hand. In the West, one looked to those sowers of the powers of significant form, the Muses. It is not the style of designation that matters: it is the affirmation, implicit and explicit, in poetry, in art, since the cave paintings of the pre-historic, of the agonistic-collaborative presence of agencies beyond the governance or conceptual grasp of the craftsman. What matters is Van Gogh's almost raging insistence that the placing of the pigment, of "the yellow that is somehow inside the shadow of the blue", is, in the severest observance of the term, a metaphysical act, an encounter with the opaque and precedent authority of essence.

In turn, it is our apprehension of this essence within but also 'behind' presentness and representation in the aesthetic which, indispensably, is the condition of trust. We yield rights of possession to the fictions of literature, to the iconic suggestions placed in us by the painter, to the life-beat of the music; we collaborate, to the best of our receptive and commemorative means, in the regeneration and perpetuation of the artist's work, precisely to the extent that we too experience the unmastered 'thereness' of a secret sharer, of a prior creation with and against which the art-act has been effected. I see no other explanation, be it, in the first instance, psychological (whatever that means), for the unseen ballast which gives a rounded density of 'real life', a presence far exceeding that of common humanity, to the *dramatis personae* of the epic, of the drama, of the novel. The word 'character' does mean the actual marker on the page. And there is undoubtedly a sense in which an Odysseus, a Falstaff, an Anna Karenina are 'characters', which is to say no more and no less than assemblages of lexical-grammatical signs on a page. But it is, very exactly, the quantum leap between the character as letter and the character as presence, and as a presence often far richer, more exigent of exploring assent, far more lasting than our own, which makes the point. Save in a formalistic sense, no sum of 'characters' creates a 'character'. The exponential modulation of the semiotic into the organic takes place in the "collision" (Hölderlin's embattled term) between the mechanics of form and the 'otherness' in meaning. Those who perceived transcendent transparency "as through a glass darkly", or urged the generation of letter into spirit, were saying the same thing, though in an idiom more immediate to the obvious than is ours.

Without some such supposition as to the felt continuities between the making of poetry and art on the one hand and the residue or re-enactment of the prior creation of being on the other, there cannot, I suggest, be any intelligible view of our inner experience of the aesthetic, nor of our free answerability to that experience. If 'characters' are only 'characters', then form is only formality and meaning only a momentary innocence or self-deception in the face of self-subverting, semantically arbitrary sign-sequences. I have tried to show that this alternative is, within its own terms, within its own ironizing rhetorical play, irrefutable. It is also, I believe, manifestly false to human experience, to that of the artist as well as to that of the receiver.

We have, for persuasive historical and psychological reasons, arrived at a point at which the natural idiom in which to state such a belief is no longer generally acceptable. Psychoanalysis, deconstruction, sceptical positivism or agnosticism of every order, very legitimately identify and feed upon this inacceptability. *Lear* allows us to phrase the radical difference. Must, as a rigorous nihilism will have it, "nothing come of nothing"? Or can we attach some substantive consequence, some weight other than that of metaphoric pathos, to the concept that the excess of wholly present but unsayable meanings in Cordelia's silence is that of art, of poetics, when these "go about their Father's business"?

In mathematics, an axiomatic system can prove its own consistency only by including at least one postulate which cannot itself be proved from within that system. Descartes wagers on the unprovable assumption that God has not devised a phenomenal universe such as to deceive human reason or such as to make impossible the recurrent application of natural laws (the deconstructive devising of such a cosmos by some 'demon of falsehood' is perfectly conceivable to logic; it is the anarchic intuition *par excellence*). Kant postulates a fundamental disposition of accord between the fabric of human understanding and our perception of things. He cannot prove this postulate. Indeed he asserts the inaccessibility of 'things in themselves' and the categorical limitations of our cognitions.

213

There is no construct, there is no intuitive imaging, of our identity in being, of our relations to the world, which does not include at least one hiatus in the chain of definition and demonstration. There is no mind-set in respect of consciousness and of 'reality' which does not make at least one leap into the dark (the *a priori*) of the unprovable.

This essay argues a wager on transcendence. It argues that there is in the art-act and its reception, that there is in the experience of meaningful form, a presumption of presence. Meaningfulness is not an invariant datum. There are indeed vacancies, deliberate or pathological 'ruptures' or spaces for 'non-sense' in otherwise intelligible modes of enunciation. But these are not of the essence. There are indeed indecipherabilities. But these also are phenomena at the margin. There is, there can be no end to interpretative disagreement and revision. But where it is seriously engaged in, the process of differing is one which cumulatively circumscribes and clarifies the disputed ground. It is, I have argued, the irreducible autonomy of presence, of 'otherness', in art and text which denies either adequate paraphrase or unanimity of finding.

These convictions are, as current linguistic philosophy puts it – when it is being polite – "verification transcendent". They cannot be logically, formally or evidentially proved. Ironic, absurdist or nihilist negation is readily to hand. So is the suspension of belief at work in liberal abstention. But let there be no mistake: such "verification transcendence" marks every essential aspect of human existence. It qualifies our conceptualizations, our intellections of our coming into life, of the primary elements of our psychic identity and instruments, of the phenomenology of Eros and of death. Scientific hypotheses and discoveries do alter the ways in which we situate, in which we articulate the constants of unknowing in our human circumstance. They may, but only to a limited extent, shift the equilibrium between the 'verification areas' and those that transcend them. The fundamental delimitation remains. It is stated, lapidarily, in Heidegger's "science does not *think*" and in the close of the *Tractatus*. Within science itself, moreover, the postulate outside proof, the leap to foundational images, is more prevalent than the layman is allowed to suppose.

The final paradox which defines our humanity prevails: there is always, there always will be, a sense in which we do not know what it is we are experiencing and talking about when we experience and talk about that which is. There is a sense in which no human discourse, however analytic, can make final sense of sense itself.

But my wager must be made more specific. I am wagering, both in a Cartesian and a Pascalian vein, on the informing pressure of a real presence in the semantic markers which generate Oedipus the King or Madame Bovary; in the pigments or incisions which externalize Grünewald's Issenheim triptych or Brancusi's *Bird*; in the notes, crotchets, markings of tempo and volume which actualize Schubert's posthumous Quintet. Generation, externalization, actualization: these are abstract verbalizations of primary comings into being of energized and signifying form from within. They are re-enactments, reincarnations via spiritual and technical means of that which human questioning, solitude, inventiveness, apprehension of time and of death can intuit of the *fiat* of creation, out of which, inexplicably, have come the self and the world into which we are cast.

Whether we would or not, these overwhelming, commonplace inexplicabilities and the imperative of questioning which is the core of man make us close neighbours to the transcendent. Poetry, art, music are the medium of that neighbourhood.

So far as it wagers on meaning, an account of the act of reading, in the fullest sense, of the act of the reception and internalization of significant forms within us, is a metaphysical and, in the last analysis, a theological one. The ascription of beauty to truth and to meaning is either a rhetorical flourish, or it is a piece of theology. It is a theology, explicit or suppressed, masked or avowed, substantive or imaged, which underwrites the presumption of creativity, of signification in our encounters with text, with music, with art. The meaning of meaning is a transcendent postulate. To read the poem responsibly ('respondingly'), to be answerable to form, is to wager on a reinsurance of sense. It is to wager on a relationship – tragic, turbulent, incommensurable, even sardonic – between word and world, but on a relationship precisely bounded by that which reinsures it. For poets, these matters are straightforward: over and over, a Dante, a Hölderlin, a Montale tell us of what poetry is saying when, exactly when, words fail it. So does the light at the Vermeer casement. And all great music.

6

Does this mean that all adult *poiesis*, that everything we recognize as being of compelling stature in literature, art, music is of a religious inspiration or reference? As a matter of history, of pragmatic inventory, the answer is almost unequivocal. Referral and self-referral to a transcendent dimension, to that which is felt to reside either explicitly – this is to say ritually, theologically, by force of revelation – or implicitly, outside immanent and purely secular reach, does underwrite created forms from Homer and the *Oresteia* to *The Brothers Karamazov* and Kafka. It informs art from the caves at Lascaux to Rembrandt and to Kandinsky. Music and the metaphysical, in the root sense of that term, music and religious feeling, have been virtually inseparable. It is in and through music that we are most immediately in the presence of the logically, of the verbally inexpressible but wholly palpable energy in being that communicates to our senses and to our reflection what little we can grasp of the naked wonder of life. I take music to be the naming of the naming of life. This is, beyond any liturgical or theological specificity, a sacramental motion. Or, as Leibniz put it: "music is a secret arithmetic of the soul unknowing of the fact that it is counting" (*nescientia se numerare*).

This is why music has been at the centre of my argument throughout. What every human being whom music moves, to whom it is a life-giving agency, can say of it is platitudinous. Music means. It is brimful of meanings which will not translate into logical structures or verbal expression. In music form is content, content form. Music is at once cerebral in the highest degree – I repeat that the energies and form-relations in the playing of a quartet, in the interactions of voice and instrument are among the most complex events known to man – and it is at the same time somatic, carnal and a searching out of resonances in our bodies at levels deeper than will or consciousness. These are banalities. Yet each and every one of them mocks analytic rationalization. Each and every one of them rebukes the arrogance of positivism, of the demand for a quantifiable, for a psychologically evidential or sociologically mapped explanation of things. We are, in respect of music, human, all too human. But intimations of a radical 'non-humanity' within music's powers, be they daemonic or consoling, exalting or desolating (and in great music they are always both), intimations of a source and destination somehow outside the range of man, have always pressed upon composer and performer. They have always persuaded the handful of philosophic sensibilities, from Plato to Schopenhauer and Nietzsche, who have had anything to say about music worth saying.

Music makes utterly substantive what I have sought to suggest of the real presence in meaning where that presence cannot be analytically shown or paraphrased. Music brings to our daily lives an immediate encounter with a logic of sense other than that of reason. It is, precisely, the truest name we have for the logic at work in the springs of being that generate vital forms. Music has celebrated the mystery of intuitions of transcendence from the songs of Orpheus, counter-creative to death, to the *Missa Solemnis*, from Schubert's late piano sonatas to Schoenberg's *Moses und Aron* and Messiaen's *Quatuor pour la fin du temps*. Countless times, this celebration has had manifest relations to religion. But the core-relation far exceeds any specific religious motive or occasion. In ways so obvious as to make any statement a tired cliché, yet of an undefinable and tremendous nature, music puts our being as men and women in touch with that which transcends the sayable, which outstrips the analysable. Music is plainly uncircumscribed by the world as the latter is an object of scientific determination and practical harnessing. The meanings of the meaning of music transcend. It has long been, it continues to be, the unwritten theology of those who lack or reject any formal creed. Or to put it reciprocally: for many human beings, religion has been the music which they believe in. In the ecstasies of Pop and of Rock, the overlap is strident.

Statistically, a rough-hewn but nevertheless undeniable marker, Western painting, sculpture and much of what is incarnate in architecture, have, until the Enlightenment, been religious and, more specifically, Scriptural, both in motivation and representational content. Epic poetry and tragic drama are articulate within a declared or simply assumed 'other-worldliness'. They are altogether inseparable from the postulate of "more things in heaven and earth". Tragedy, in particular – and it may be, until now, the most eloquent, concentratedly questioning of all aesthetic genres – is God-haunted from Aeschylus to Claudel. It posits man unhoused at those crossroads where the mystery of his condition is made naked to the ambiguous intercessions of menace and of grace. There is, as Socrates hints, a corollary in the *tristia* of high comedy. The gods are most present in their hiddenness when they smile. Witness Feste's song in *Twelfth Night*, the mortal laughter at the close of Mozart's enigmatic *Così fan tutte*, or Chekhov's valedictions.

The vehicle is, more often than not, that of myth. Myth contains a fundamental extra-territoriality to finitude. This is an awkward tag, but, I think, indispensable. A positivist cosmology, because it would tie 'strings' (the latest mathematical-imagistic device in the quest for a General Theory) around the universe, is finite. Theories, crucial experiments, algebraic models aim at proof. Proof is, in essence, terminal. Even at infinity – itself a precise, technical concept – there is end-stopping. But the humblest of myths, on the contrary, is open-ended. The inference of trans-rational possibility in all authentic mythical forms – theirs is, indeed, "the music of what happens" – is no archaic indulgence. Myth offers to our impatient questioning the most vivid perception of the neighbourhood to our everyday experience of the 'otherness' in life and in death. In ancient literatures and art, the religious and the mythical are fused under the common rubric of the mythological. The truth-functions of the revealed in Christianity, such as Transubstantiation and Resurrection, lead a double life. They are, at once, and for the literalist believer, narratives of verity; and they are the *translatio*, the 'carrying-over' of systematic inexplicability into the more elusive, intermittent and self-querying inexplicability of mythical narration. Observe how this dynamic of 'translation' – again Bottom is our witness – of the modulation from postulated form into free form is itself inherent in what meanings we are able or willing to attach to the passage of real presence into bread and wine in the one instance, and to the reversion of death into life in the other.

Elsewhere, the relations between the literary text, musical composition or painting whose motifs are mythical and the transcendent core or sub-text are more oblique. The distinctions to be made can be seen, in shorthand, as those which obtain between, say, Wagner's *Ring* and *Parsifal*. The welding of myth to religion is seamless in Victor Hugo's late epics on God and on Satan. It is beautifully angular in Faulkner's *Light in August*. In Melville's *Moby Dick*, in the parable of the Grand Inquisitor in *The Brothers Karamazov*, the metamorphic energies of the myth-fiction almost appropriate to themselves the authority, the reinsuring centrality of the scriptural-theological source. Even within a domestic, secular genre, which is that of the modern novel, the great exemplars continue to ask, aloud or beneath their breath (as in Proust), the one question ineradicable in man: Is there or is there not God? Is there or is there not meaning to being?

It is the potential of myth to make of the *mysterium*, of the 'irrationality' of its religious background something that is "rich and strange" in another way. I have been calling it the 'inexplicable' in the dark light of Franz Kafka's definition of myth in his parable on Prometheus. Others might call it heresy or erosion. In the rococo, in the Enlightenment, in certain nineteenth-century uses of myth, there is a suppression of the numinous, of the supernatural concession. Symbol is flattened to form, a flattening against which the turbulent upward rushes in the art of a Tiepolo are an ambivalent protest. The mythical, as it were, survives its content. Or it is, as in the Freudian readings, psychologized, made not infinitely inward but internal (in the sense in which we speak of 'internal medicine'). Sophocles'

Oedipus makes inexplicable what may have been the more ritually transparent enigma of the myth. It is in this deepening of the unacceptable, in this 'abyssality', that lies the seed and surge of tragedy. Freud's misreading of Sophocles, itself deliberately generative of a therapeutic myth, flattens. It severs the life of the mind and of feeling not only from the unrecapturable religious-ritual source, but from that never-to-be-exhausted abstention from explanation, from finite paraphrase, which is the acting-out, the substantiation of the myth as we know it in the play.

The equivocations, that word out of the spectral terrors in *Macbeth*, between finite, liberal rationality after "the death of God" on the one hand, and the questionings of immanence which are radical to myth on the other, have been of peculiar intensity throughout modernism. No period since the early Renaissance has been more concerned with, has addressed itself more insistently to, the nature of the mythical than our own. Re-mythologization in a time which has found agnostic secularism more or less unendurable may, in future, be seen as defining the spirit of the age. The motion from T. S. Eliot's *The Waste Land* to the *Four Quartets* is schematic of a progress, if it is that, from the *terra incognita* of the mythical to the mastered unknown of a systematic and doctrinal vision. Christology as myth underlies Pasternak's *Doctor Zhivago* no less than Beckett's grieving satires on the messianic. Picasso makes of his prodigal citations and representations of ancient myths 'illustrations'. In one sense, these, like their eighteenth- and nineteenth-century precedent, defuse, even mock the pressures of transcendence in the primal fable. But in another way, the Minotaur sequence being an awesome case in point, Picasso's images mask, transparently, an undenied riddle and terror of presence. If Joyce's *Ulysses* is an attempt, perhaps the most inspiredly willed and pedantic that we have, to ground myth in mundanity, to bring to earth the numinous aura of the mythological, Thomas Mann's Joseph trilogy and Hermann Broch's *Death of Virgil* would invest in prose fiction the burdens of revelation characteristic of religion and the openness to unknowing distinctive of myth.

Of special fascination is the devolution from religion to mysticism, from the theological to the esoteric, in Dada, in Surrealism, in current schools of non-objective and non-representational art. As early as May 1917, Hans Arp helped launch Dada by reading publicly from Jakob Boehme's theosophic speculations, in his *Aurora* of 1612, on the gnostic interplay between light and dark. Time and again, Cubism cites the notion, formulated by Blavatsky, of "the geometries of God". Kandinsky's *On the Spiritual in Art* is a profoundly religious manifesto. As if in terror of the emptiness, of the vacancies with which it was so intimate – that "great emptiness" within which and against which Yves Klein pitches his paintings – abstract art strives "to make visible the invisible world". It is neo-Platonic in its mystique of light, of the "immense arc of light which touches the earth and makes it sing" (Arp). No less than the virtuosi of contemplation in Patristic and medieval Christianity, constructivist painting and sculpture immerses itself in *"le blanc infini"*, the boundlessness of pure white light and of significant emptiness (*blanc* means both). In 1924, Kurt Schwitters went so far as to define Dada, with its absurdist unworldliness, with its protest against social injustice and war, as "the spirit of Christianity in the realm of art". "The artist", wrote Barnett Newman in the mid 1940s, "tries to wrest truth from the void." The dialectic between blank and form, between the unmaking of the representational and its reconstitution, is played out between Mondrian and Anselm Kiefer. In a sequence of riveting studies, Mondrian deconstructs a tree into purely abstract markers of linearity; in *Piet Mondrian's*

Arminius' Battle, painted in 1976, Kiefer shows a great tree, a 'Tree of Man' and one upon which hangs the absent weight of the 'Son of Man', re-emerging, gathering form and our consciousness of form out of "the great emptiness".

As there is trivial, opportunistic literature and music, so there is modern art which is mere shadow-boxing, which only mimes, with more or less technical *brio*, a genuine struggle with emptiness. There are bricks piled on museum floors and strips of torn sacking on modish walls. The great role occupied by the esoteric, the part of Zen, of the Kabbalistic, of the shaman in, for example, the genius of American Abstract Expressionism, tells directly of the difficulties which the artist faces when he seeks for an idiom truthful to his creative experience in a society, in a moment of history where the frankly theological is so largely held in derision. Where a rationality modelled, naïvely, on that of the sciences and of technology prevails, where agnosticism, if not a consequent atheism, is the norm of approved discourse, it is immensely difficult for an artist to find words for his making, for the "vibrations of the primal" which quicken his work. Pervasively, however, major art in our vexed modernity has been, like all great shaping before it, touched by the fire and the ice of God.

One asks: Can there be a secular poetics in the strict sense? Can there be an understanding of that which engenders 'texts' and which makes their reception possible which is not underwritten by a postulate of transcendence, by Plato's "aspiration to invisible reality"?

On the face of it, the question looks foolish. An immense range of literature, music, fine art has been manifestly worldly in reference and intent. Surely, literature has never ceased to celebrate the joys and sorrows, the enchantments and ridicule, of the matter of matter. The vast majority of song and dance is

223

just that: it paces the works and days, the needs, the sabbatical hours of common mortality. In what possible regard – except, and this is vital still, in so far as a painter's or sculptor's impulse is counter-creative – can we attach transcendent dimensions to the still-life, to the portrait, to the numberless depictions of the natural and domestic settings in which we lead our non-metaphysical lives? The sensuality of the acceptance of the finite world, by which I would want to define both laughter and tolerance, is the context and content not only of a major portion of aesthetic constructs, but of that kind of experience which the evident majority of readers, listeners, viewers look to when they turn to music, art or literature.

An investment in the sublime, in the *opus metaphysicum* may flatter the critic, the interpreter-scholar. It may compensate for his own (my own) limitations of creative power. Nevertheless. Can a logic of immanence account for the coming into being of the fact of meaningful form? A triple echo may be of help. The precept is in Augustine; the rephrasing is by Boehme; it is Coleridge who transcribes: "I warn all Inquirers into this hard point to *wait* – not only not to plunge forward before the Word is *given* to them, but not even to paw the ground with impatience. For in a deep stillness only can this truth be apprehended." *Datur, non intelligitur.* There is no mysticism in this monition; only the elusive light of common sense.

For it is a plain fact that, most certainly in the West, the writings, works of art, musical compositions which are of central reference, comport that which is "grave and constant" (Joyce's epithets) in the mystery of our condition. There was, presumably, no need of books or of art in Eden. That which has been indispensable thereafter has communicated the urgency of a great hurt. It is in the perspective of death – how *can* we die, how are we able to? – that Western consciousness has spoken,

has sung its realizations of love and of *caritas*. A "high seriousness" of questioning and immateriality, in the true sense of that
most radical word, inhabits what we recognize as lasting in the
acts of art and in our readings of them. The political bestiality of
our times, the social injustice, the rape of the natural world,
make this habitation at once decisive and problematic.

I am arguing that the 'gravity' and the 'constancy' are, finally,
religious. As is the category of meaningfulness. They are
religious in two main senses. The first is obvious. The *Oresteia*,
King Lear, Dostoevsky's *The Devils* no less than the art of Giotto
or the Passions of Bach, inquire into, dramatize, the relations of
man and woman to the existence of the gods or of God. It is the
Hebraic intuition that God is capable of all speech-acts except
that of monologue which has generated our arts of reply, of
questioning and counter-creation. After the Book of Job and
Euripides' *Bacchae*, there *had* to be, if man was to bear his being,
the means of dialogue with God which are spelt out in our
poetics, music, art.

The gravity and constancy at the heart of major forms and of
our understanding of them are religious in a second, more
diffuse sense. They enact, as I have noted, a root-impulse of the
human spirit to explore possibilities of meaning and of truth that
lie outside empirical seizure or proof. Pre-eminent in this *moto
spirituale* is the inference, either implicit or explicit, of the
preternatural agency, of the borderland. So very much in
Western art and literature enlists the proposal that we are close
neighbours to the unknown, that we move among orders of
pragmatic substance themselves permeable to that which lies on
the other side, which acts from beyond 'the shadow-line'. There
can be no *Odyssey* without its descent among the clairvoyant
dead; no Hamlet without the Ghost. But there can also be no
Remembrance of Things Past without Proust's summons of the

death-Angels whose wings infold with the leaves of the master-works of the dead craftsmen. Serious music, art, literature, in their own wager on survivance, are refusals of analytic-empirical criteria of constraint. Always, the artist and his respondent know, with Sir Thomas Browne, "that we are men and we know not how; there is something in us that can be without us, nor cannot tell how it entered into us".

The artist and poet and musician translate this insight into living and lived form. Theirs is the metaphysical assumption, where the metaphysical also extends to the religious. The "verification transcendence" which this entails is a discipline of unknowing. Be it in a specifically religious, for us Judaeo-Christian sense, or in the more general Platonic-mythological guise, the aesthetic is the making formal of epiphany. There is a "shining through".

In the *Paradiso*, Dante tells of an arrow striking home before the music of the bow string has ceased. The *vibrato* persists inside us after the sound. That durance may be as near as we can come to the speculative intimation that there are values and energies in the human person – and *per-sonare* means, precisely, a 'sounding' a 'saying through' – which transcend death. Access to such an intimation is, in the light of reason and of the scientific, puerile mumbo-jumbo. What we can say, a saying both exceeding and falling short of responsible knowledge, is that there is music which conveys both the grave constancy, the finality of death and a certain refusal of that very finality. This dual motion, instinctual to humanity but scandalous to reason, is evident, it is made transparent to spiritual, intellectual and physical notice, in Schubert's C-major Quintet. Listen to the slow movement.

To summarize: it is, I believe, poetry, art and music which relate us most directly to that in being which is not ours. Science is no less animate in its making of models and images. But these are not, finally, disinterested. They aim at mastery, at ownership. It is counter-creation and counter-love, as these are embodied in the aesthetic and in our reception of formed meaning, which put us in sane touch with that which transcends, with matters 'undreamt of' in our materiality. The limits of our language are not, *pace* Wittgenstein, those of our world (and as a man immersed in music, he knew that). The arts are most wonderfully rooted in substance, in the human body, in stone, in pigment, in the twanging of gut or the weight of wind on reeds. All good art and literature begin in immanence. But they do not stop there. Which is to say, very plainly, that it is the enterprise and privilege of the aesthetic to quicken into lit presence the continuum between temporality and eternity, between matter and spirit, between man and 'the other'. It is in this common and exact sense that *poiesis* opens on to, is underwritten by, the religious and the metaphysical. The questions: 'What is poetry, music, art?', 'How can they not be?', 'How do they act upon us and how do we interpret their action?', are, ultimately, theological questions.

7

I have, before, cited some of those who know best: the poets, the artists. I have found no deconstructionist among them. I have found none who can, in conscience, accept the constraints on permissible discourse prescribed by logical atomism, logical positivism, scientific proof-values or, in a far more pervasive sense, by liberal scepticism. Despite the psychoanalytic demonstration, itself foreshadowed by Hume, by Feuerbach and by Marx, that religious propositions are illusory phantasms which originate in infantilism and neurosis, the makers do not seem to be listening. (The one great exception may be that of Leopardi.) D. H. Lawrence's is a summarizing statement: "I always feel as if I stood naked for the fire of Almighty God to go through me – and it's rather an awful feeling. One has to be so terribly religious to be an artist." And there is Yeats: "No man can create as did Shakespeare, Homer, Sophocles, who does not believe with all his blood and nerve, that man's soul is immortal." And quotation could continue. Wittily, Bertrand Russell asserted that God had simply given to man far too few indices of His existence for religious faith to be plausible. Yet this observation is, meta-physically, tone-deaf. It leaves out the entire sphere of the poetic, be it metaphysical or aesthetic, it leaves out music and the arts, without which human life might indeed not be viable.

I know that this formulation will be unacceptable not only to most of those who will read a book such as this, but also to the prevailing climate of thought and of feeling in our culture. It is just this unacceptability which characterizes what I have called a time of 'epilogue', an immanence within the logic of the 'afterword'. The notion that there is some fundamental encounter with transcendence in the creation of art and in its experiencing ebbs from educated trust well before Matthew Arnold declares this ebbing. At most, and with justified suspicion, current sentiment may allow Wallace Stevens's proposal that "After one has abandoned a belief in God, poetry is the essence which takes its place as life's redemption." Today, sensibility concedes a certain "emptiness in the desert of reason" (Hegel), but such emptiness and the thirst it may provoke are held to be far preferable to the bromides or outright venom of dead creeds. Politically, morally perhaps, little, very little in this twentieth century, one of the cruellest, most wasteful of hope in human record, gives motive for anything but a lucid 'forgetting about' God.

In recent art and thought, it is not a forgetting which is instrumental, but a negative theism, a peculiarly vivid sense of God's absence or, to be precise, of His recession. The 'other' has withdrawn from the incarnate, leaving either uncertain secular spoors or an emptiness which echoes still with the vibrance of departure. Our aesthetic forms explore the void, the blank freedom which come of the retraction (*Deus absconditus*) of the messianic and the divine. If the "hallowed precision" of Georges de La Tour's *Job Mocked by his Wife* at Epinal or of a Giorgione landscape enact the epiphany of a real presence, if they proclaim the kinship of art with the calling on mystery in the matter of the world and of man, a Malevich, an Ad Reinhardt reveal, with no less authority, their encounter with a 'real absence'. So, we have seen, do post-structuralism and deconstruction. Within Derridean readings lies a "zero theology" of the "always absent". The *Ur*-text is 'there', but made insignificant by a primordial act of absence. We think of that Torah imagined by certain Kabbalists, of a meaningfulness untouched by human speech, by human ambiguities of reference or interpretation and, therefore, out of reach.

It is 'in this absence' that we shadow-box or, as German so aptly puts it, 'fence against mirrors'.

What I affirm is the intuition that where God's presence is no longer a tenable supposition and where His absence is no longer a felt, indeed overwhelming weight, certain dimensions of thought and creativity are no longer attainable. And I would vary Yeats's axiom so as to say: no man can read fully, can answer answeringly to the aesthetic, whose 'nerve and blood' are at peace in sceptical rationality, are now at home in immanence and verification. We must read *as if*.

The density of God's absence, the edge of presence in that absence, is no empty dialectical twist. The phenomenology is elementary: it is like the recession from us of one whom we have loved or sought to love or of one before whom we have dwelt in fear. The distancing is, then, charged with the pressures of a nearness out of reach, of a remembrance torn at the edges. It is this absent 'thereness', in the death-camps, in the laying waste of a grimed planet, which is articulate in the master-texts of our age. It lies in Kafka's parables, in the namings of Golgotha in Beckett's *Endgame*, in the Psalms to No-one of Paul Celan. It is, to reverse Kierkegaard's phrase, where the helper is no longer the help, but one still resonant with recent receding, that the futile light flashes on the execution of Joseph K., that Beckett's Malone lurches into nullity.

It is only when the question of the existence or non-existence of God will have lost all actuality, it is only when, as logical positivism teaches, it will have been recognized and felt to be strictly nonsensical, that we shall inhabit a scientific-secular world. Educated opinion has, to a greater or lesser degree, entered upon this new freedom. For it, emptiness is precisely and only that. General sentiment may follow; or it may, most threateningly, aspire to religious fundamentalism and *kitsch* ideologies.

It may well be that the forgetting of the question of God will be the nub of cultures now nascent. It may be that the verticalities of reference to 'higher things', to the impalpable and mythical which are still incised in our grammars, which are still the ontological guarantors of the arcs of metaphor, will drain from speech (consider the 'languages' of the computer and the codes in artificial intelligence). Should these mutations of consciousness and expression come into force, the forms of aesthetic making as we have known them will no longer be productive. They will be relegated to historicity. Correspondingly, the modes of response, of hermeneutic encounter as I have outlined

230

them, will become archaeologies. Philology will no longer know a *Logos* for its love. I have adverted to the fact that so large a measure of contemporary musical performance and audition, of what is seen in the museum, of what is canonic in textuality, already looks to the past. The humanist, in crucial contrast to the scientist, tends to feel that both dawn and noon are at his back.

Such conjectures cannot be proven. The discrimination I have proposed throughout is formulated in Aristotle's *Metaphysics*: "It is a matter of *apaideusis* not to distinguish between that which requires demonstration or proof and that which does not." *Apaideusis* can be translated as meaning a want of schooling, a fundamental lesion in education. I would render the term as connoting an indecency of spirit and of understanding.

If my general intuition has substance, indifference to the theological and the metaphysical, to the question of whether or not the confines of the pragmatic and of the logically and experimentally falsifiable are or are not those of human existentiality, will mean a radical break with aesthetic creation and reception. Where it is genuinely immanent – and I am by no means certain that I know what this would mean – the poetics, the art of the 'after-Word' and the interpretative responses they will solicit, will be essentially different from those we have known and whose after-life prevails still, though often either trivialized or made mandarin, in today's transitional circumstances.

There is one particular day in Western history about which neither historical record nor myth nor Scripture make report. It is a Saturday. And it has become the longest of days. We know of that Good Friday which Christianity holds to have been that of the Cross. But the non-Christian, the atheist, knows of it as well. This is to say that he knows of the injustice, of the interminable suffering, of the waste, of the brute enigma of ending, which so largely make up not only the historical dimension of the human condition, but the everyday fabric of our personal lives. We know, ineluctably, of the pain, of the failure of love, of the solitude which are our history and private fate. We know also about Sunday. To the Christian, that day signifies an intimation, both assured and precarious, both evident and beyond comprehension, of resurrection, of a justice and a love that have conquered death. If we are non-Christians or non-believers, we know of that Sunday in precisely analogous terms. We conceive of it as the day of liberation from inhumanity and servitude. We look to resolutions, be they therapeutic or political, be they social or messianic. The lineaments of that Sunday carry the name of hope (there is no word less deconstructible).

But ours is the long day's journey of the Saturday. Between suffering, aloneness, unutterable waste on the one hand and the dream of liberation, of rebirth on the other. In the face of the torture of a child, of the death of love which is Friday, even the greatest art and poetry are almost helpless. In the Utopia of the Sunday, the aesthetic will, presumably, no longer have logic or necessity. The apprehensions and figurations in the play of metaphysical imagining, in the poem and the music, which tell of pain and of hope, of the flesh which is said to taste of ash and of the spirit which is said to have the savour of fire, are always Sabbatarian. They have risen out of an immensity of waiting which is that of man. Without them, how could we be patient?

INDEX